MW01698023

"Dr. Mark Tubbs has both the experience and wisdom to write a book on the apostolic ministry of today! You'll want share this with your pastor and friends. *Relational Transformation* will leave you with a greater understanding of the apostolic, its function today in the church, and how it applies to your life. I've known Mark for many years and traveled with him and seen first hand the gift that operates in his life. Read it and find a practical guide for you and for your ministry!"

BRIAN SIMMONS
The Passion Translation Project

"Mark and Ann Tubbs are senior leaders in the HIM - Harvest International Ministry movement, with churches and ministries in 60 countries. It is out of this experience that *Relational Transformation* has been was birthed. This book is not a teaching devoid of application. Rather, this book has the power to unite us around the true heart and purpose of an apostle. As friends and co-laborers with Mark and Ann we have seen the fruit of *Relational Transformation* first hand. In countries around the world this teaching has sown the seeds of transformation to produce measurable fruit. This book is a must for any leader that wants to bring those around them into relationships that launch them into their destiny. It also provides clarity on how God is moving apostolically today, and how everyone can be a part of it!

WESLEY AND STACEY CAMPBELL
Founders, Be a Hero & Eyes and Wings

"Salvation by faith is today recognized as a core element of Christianity. However for many centuries it was lost to the Church and at last restored in an era known as the Reformation. Today is a momentous time, as God is revealing another long lost treasure that has been hidden for centuries: the apostolic. The rediscovery of this function in the Body of Christ holds immense potential for the advance of the Gospel in these latter days. *Relational Transformation* is a timely work that reveals the awesome potential for transformed lives when everyday people allow God to use them in apostolic ways.

What does 'apostolic' mean? How should it be practiced today in alignment with Scripture? *Relational Transformation* will answer these questions. Dr. Mark Tubbs is a the most qualified person I know to write a practical guidebook on apostolic fatherhood and transformation of lives. He regularly visits our ministry field in north India and I've had the intense privilege of ministering alongside this true apostolic father. Mark will take you into his own discovery and practice of the apostolic...and will empower you to flow in the apostolic as well! Get ready to go to a new level of personal fulfillment and global influence. *Relational Transformation* will prepare you to be a vessel that God can use apostolically to transform lives, communities and nations!"

DR. LEANNA CINQUANTA
Director, TellAsia Ministries

"As I read Mark Tubbs new book, *Relational Transformation*, I couldn't help but wish I had read it decades earlier. In a very real transparent way Mark shares his journey into Apostolic ministry. His writings are filled with insight, honesty, and hope. I enthusiastically recommend this book to anyone seeking to understand or become more involved in ministry that is both Biblical as well as practical."

MARK ESTES
North Palm Church
North Charleston Apostolic Center

"Prepare to resonate with this refreshingly authentic account of Mark Tubb's growth into God's call on his life. If, like me, you are navigating a transition into a bigger story, this book will help you gain greater clarity in your destiny and design with practical tools and thought provoking stories. In a few short chapters, 'Papa Mark' provides insight and mentoring to launch you in your character, your five-fold gifting, and to assist you in creating an atmosphere where people around you flourish. This is a must-read book for apostles in training, and a practical guide for spiritual parenting/mentoring, alignment, and equipping for transformation of cities and nations. Ralph Waldo Emerson said, 'In each pause I hear the call.' Take the time to pause and read this book. God has a call for you."

MATT WEAVER
The River Church, Senior Leader
Portal School of Creativity & Innovation, Co-Founder
Crystal River Estate Management, CEO

"Mark and Ann Tubbs are world changers who come as servants and friends who bring the Father's love into your life. With humor and humility, Mark brings us into his journey from a local Baptist pastor to a global apostolic ambassador. He traces the steps of his transformation, the confusion of not fitting in, the surprises and the 'aha moments' of recognizing the Holy Spirit's work as he learned to flow in apostolic function. It's all real, transparent, and accessible through honest stories that will engage your attention and encourage your heart. This book is full of encouragement, practical equipping and inspiration."

DR. CHARLES STOCK
Senior Leader, Life Center Ministries International
Harrisburg, Pennsylvania

"Go on a journey with my friend, Mark Tubbs, as he pioneers territory that is foreign to some but not this dear man of God. As an experienced scout and spiritual encourager, he can navigate trails unknown to you and help you walk into apostolic realms you were destined to possess. You can trust the teachings in this ground breaking book."

JAMES W. GOLL
Founder of God Encounters Ministries
International Speaker & Author

RELATIONAL
TRANSFORMATION

Fathering, Alignment + The Apostolic

DR. MARK D. TUBBS, PHD

RELATIONAL
TRANSFORMATION

By Dr. Mark Tubbs

Cover and book layout design by Westerly Creative.

Published by Reign by Rain,
Los Angeles, CA.

ACKNOWLEDGMENTS

What would a book called, "*Relational Transformation*" be without honoring the relationships in my life? First and foremost, it begins with an amazing God who calls me by name. He is the source and inspiration for all that I am and experience. Thank you, Lord, for creating me and setting me a part in the womb for Your purpose. May all glory be given to Jesus!

Secondly, my wife, Ann, is not only supportive, she is the ultimate in a life-partner and friend. Ann carries a faith-filled heart for the Lord Jesus, and her pursuit of His presence impacts me and thousands of others around the world. Our marriage has taught me about God's love, and our unity unfolds our lives and destinies. While she has her own gifts and ministry, she has always been there for me. She has sacrificed her dreams at times and served beside me as we pour into churches around the world. Ann's consistency in prayer has brought us through, and upholds all that we are and do.

My three natural children, Loraina, and the twins, Kevin and Marcus, are an inspiration and joy to my life. Each one has different characteristics and is brilliant in their own way. I treasure them and continue to pray that they will come into the fullness of God's purpose. This year we have gained two more family members by marriage, Glen and Amy. I love them deeply and look forward to what we will share together.

As I look over our years in ministry (serving in three local churches during a span of 24 years, and now with

Harvest International Ministry for 12), there are thousands of people that have impacted my life directly. I mention many by name in this book, so I won't do that here. However, I want to thank the countless unnamed people that have loved me and been a part of the journey. Thank you to all my spiritual sons and daughters, and those who have called me, "Papa," or honored me as one. In our role, leaders from churches and ministries open their hearts to us and invite us in like family; they receive us as their own. Thank you for being among those who have done this.

My parents are very supportive. In fact, my step-father (who is a "Papa" to me), John Kennelly, is the primary editor of this book. Thank you, Big John! My mother, Barbara, and parents, Don and Pat Tubbs, have enthusiastically cheered us on and pray regularly as we travel the nations.

My daughter, Loraina, is an active partner in this publishing endeavor as an editor, graphic designer, and book title censor! Actually, we are putting this book under her business label, Reign by Rain, and Ann and I will do many more projects and life together with her.

It is important to thank Ché and Sue Ahn, and the HIM family under their leadership. I speak a great deal about the Ahn's in this book. It is their commitment to God, family, and others like us that are at the foundations of our journey. We feel deeply loved and honored.

Lastly, I want to thank you, the reader, and those who received my first book on the fivefold. It is my heart to impact your life, and I am grateful that hungry ones as yourself have been a crucial part of this entire process.

Grateful and Blessed,
Mark Tubbs

TABLE OF CONTENTS

PREFACE

The English language is a funny thing, as in "funny strange." We think we are saying the same thing when we use similar words, but the truth is they can have very different meanings. As the Body of Christ, we share a vital and fundamental language. At the same time we can have very different views while almost using identical words. The words "apostle" and "apostolic" are such words that stir up varying ideas and viewpoints.

As churches grow and change, there are new participants and members that join looking to be a part. When people come, it would be ideal if they had a clean slate, but the reality is that there are always old leanings even if one cannot identify where the ideas originated.

The purpose of this book is to strengthen and equip the Body of Christ in this current generation. I have the privilege of being an overseer and leader that speaks and brings teachings to new and developing churches around the world. In part, this book is really to support them. It is to be used as a tool to help communicate with new members the essence of what we mean by using the words "apostolic" and the "fivefold ministry." Our heart is not to isolate the "important" people and give them titles, but to create a community that releases people into their purpose and to train and encourage leaders to become master equippers in accordance with Ephesians 4:12.

Another purpose is to alleviate confusion, misrepresentation, and lack of clarity when it comes to the role of the apostolic for today. Through the sharing of our story and journey, it is intended to be an autobiography in a sense; to give people an example of what it looks like in practical application. We often have only theories, so it is helpful to have real and concrete expressions that verify and bolster our tenets of truth.

When it comes down to it, we need a "*Relational Transformation*." This requires a new paradigm of how we relate to one another in the Kingdom of God. This is about how we relate to others, especially if we are leaders and we want to impact people's lives. In these pages you will discover how apostolic ministry impacts relationships, and gain practical understanding and counsel on how to function as spiritual parents and operate in alignment.

Through my own process of relational transformation, I have learned a great deal from my personal apostles, Ché and Sue Ahn, along with other role models with whom we have sojourned in the service of our Lord Jesus. I bear witness to their humility, strength of character, sacrificial giving, and freedom of expression. To my benefit, these traits are indeed contagious. Through our connection with them, we have had a *Relational Transformation* in our lives. It is an honor for Ann and me to be a part of something much bigger than ourselves. I believe that is what most people want, and that is why this book is an invitation into a global movement. It is my hope that this book will be effective in unlocking the apostolic ministry into many lives.

FOREWORD

By Dr. Ché Ahn

As the Apostle, Founder and President of HIM (Harvest International Ministry), an apostolic network of networks, I can safely say that there need to be more books like *Relational Transformation*, this latest offering of HIM Missions Apostle, Mark Tubbs. Mark explains in a clear and relatable way the power and practicality of apostolic ministry today and its ability to bring transformation and reformation, from small villages to cities and nations. Mark rightly discerns that the church has been too long inwardly focused, and it is the job of the apostolic ministry to release people into their destinies and rightful authority so that the church can go out and bring lasting Kingdom change.

Mark and Ann Tubbs have been in covenant relationship with Sue and I for over a decade now, as they joined HIM in 2004 and were commissioned as apostles in 2006. In that time, Mark has served as the Executive Director of HIM and has been released into even greater global effectiveness as the Missions Apostle for Harvest International Ministry. Mark and Ann can not only speak about the ability for apostolic ministry to spark spiritual growth, shifting, and transformation, but they have lived it as they were themselves baptized into this new wine paradigm which transformed the Baptist church they had been leading at that time into a community that operated in prophecy, miracles, and apostolic outreach to Kenya.

Mark's passion for equipping and releasing people into their divine calling is tangible, whether he is speaking to pastors in the United States or churches, businesspersons, or leaders in need of training throughout the nations of the world. His gifting and authority as an apostle inspires and enables people to identify their fivefold anointing and do the work of ministry in all seven spheres of society and culture. This is how true transformation and reformation of culture happens—when we begin to minster outside of the four walls of the church.

Relational Transformation gives a clear and practical understanding of how God has been operating in the nations through the apostolic ministry. Mark uses his own prophetic journey of discovery and stepping into anointing and destiny to illumine what it looks like when we lean 100 percent on the Lord and walk out our callings and gifting. *Relational Transformation* is an encouraging book with practical application throughout for anyone looking to understand how their fivefold anointing operates within an apostolic culture.

DR. CHÉ AHN
President, Harvest International Ministry
Founding Pastor, HRock Church, Pasadena, CA
International Chancellor, Wagner University

PART I:

THE FOUNDATIONS OF RELATIONAL TRANSFORMATION

1

A GLOBAL MOVEMENT

My wife Ann and I have a rare opportunity in the body of Christ. We get to interact and encourage churches in nations all over the world. During 2016, we went to 15 different nations and met with leaders on five continents. My purpose in sharing this is not to boast, but to let you know that we are seeing the powerful hand of the Spirit moving with our own eyes. In the following pages I want to share that we are living in an amazing season as the Church around the world.

As a local church pastor for more than 24 years, I know how easy it is to feel isolated and separated from other churches. It takes a lot of work and focus to maintain a church, let alone have it grow. To reach out to other churches in the city and beyond takes navigation and wisdom. In addition, there are many barriers to real unity, beside the common wedges of theology. Deterrents such as timing, styles, priorities, and busyness come against us and are a hindrance to the cause of working together. During the past several years it has been so encouraging to hear from others what God was doing! With great joy I am telling you that there is a movement of God that is transforming the world. We don't hear these reports from the media, but there are places on earth where Christianity is exploding and growing at rates beyond imagination.

In this book, I am asking you to step back for a moment

with me and marvel at God's plan for salvation and healing the world He loves. Since we're dealing with imperfect human beings, the Church likewise isn't perfect, we can list many ways that our differences alienate the world around us. But, that doesn't change the fact that the Spirit is working in a mighty way. As we go to the different nations, I sense the growing confidence that God is answering our prayers for breakthrough and lasting change. In other words, there is a measurable global movement that is having a sustainable impact on many hot spots.

In truth, there are concurrent movements and diverse expressions of the Hand of God touching people. For certain, I don't lay claim to be the only part of the movement as I recognize that the Lord is working in many different ways through unique and unusual peoples. However, there is a movement that is identifiable and has characteristics that are consistent with the early church found in the book of Acts.

In contrast to a history lesson with lots of names and dates, I believe it will be more helpful to simply share our story about how we have been impacted by this move of God. In the course of this, it will be easy to name significant people in this stream of believers. The goal, however, is not to give all the specifics, but more to share what is happening and what it means to be a part of this movement in a real way. This is a story about a relational transformation in the context of the movement.

Our Story of Transition

Ann and I were pastors of a local church for over 10 years when we "hit a wall." We were a part of a Baptist denomination, and were at three different churches during that time span. During that decade we never witnessed or even really sought a miracle or healing. We were not against them really, we just were not in a culture that encouraged moving in the supernatural. Certainly there were "miracles" through God's faithfulness and love, but nothing that shouted out or pointed to the nine spiritual gifts listed in 1 Corinthians 12.

I share a testimony of physical healing in my first book, entitled "The Five Fingers of God." It took place in 1995 when a woman from our church asked us to pray for her healing of cervical cancer. When she asked us to pray, something happened inside. I felt powerless and inadequate. It was an overwhelming feeling I will never forget. Here we were, pastoring a church, even seeing growth while we were doing all that we were taught to do. Doing what we were taught to do was the problem. The truth is that we often think that this is all we can do; to merely follow through with what we know and with what is familiar. We would likely change if we knew how to change and the steps necessary to do so.

Without thinking I exclaimed "Why don't you try another church that knows how to pray for healing?" She took me up on that encouragement and she visited a Vineyard church nearby. The following Sunday at the end of the service, the pastor declared, "The Spirit is telling me that there is a woman here that has cancer in her womb, and that God wants to heal her today. Her issue is that she has had an abortion, and God wants to not only heal her physically, but also wants to heal her heart." (Quotes are used here, but the statement is paraphrased to express the intent). The woman went forward in faith, believing that God had revealed her situation and secret for the purpose of healing. That is exactly what happened; she had a powerful encounter with God. She experienced physical healing and emotional comfort in a way she had never experienced before.

When she reported back to us, we were amazed and

challenged to say the least. I called the pastor with sincerity, and asked him how he heard that so specifically. He explained and shared with me how it happened, and that it was through a "word of knowledge" by the Holy Spirit. Then he offered to come and train us as how to hear God in the same way.

I want to underscore something here. All of us who are Christians are a part of a facet of the body of Christ. (Romans 12:4). While each believer and church is unique, we can generally trace our roots into a historical expression of the Christian faith. With or without knowing it, our essential tenets and core values can be found in different groups that proceed us. We can use the metaphor of a tree with its many branches to illustrate that our current theological beliefs are influenced by movements from the past. While all branches are connected ultimately to the trunk, they are not necessarily connected to each other. These differences are to be a strength to the body, but often these dissimilarities are used against others that causes division.

A Stream flowing Into a River

In the story above, it reveals that our Baptist church was not at all Charismatic. Yet the Charismatic movement impacted us and changed us forever. We didn't choose to reject our past, but like a mountain stream running downhill, we flowed into a large river that we had never seen or been a part of before. This is what a movement is. It is illustrated by a large river that gathers people from many smaller and various streams and unites them and takes them to an altogether different place. That is how it happened to us.

However, we did not understand at the time that the Charismatic movement actually had many streams and also many rivers that branched out and went different ways. Again, my goal here is not to get too bound up in history, but it is important to mention that one very significant movement of God was happening around the world circa 1994. Some called this move the "Toronto Blessing," as that was one of the main fountainheads of this move. A church of 300 in Toronto received a prophetic word that they were going to help renew the entire body of Christ. Can you imagine getting such a word? It would be very hard to believe.

Yet, the Airport Vineyard Church in Toronto, Canada, did exactly that. Under the leadership of John and Carol Arnott, the church hosted people from all around the world with protracted meetings. The purpose was to renew the church and experience a release of the Father's Blessing of love. This move did not start in Toronto, but the city and church became a focal point or nucleus. Many nations were represented with visitors and it was a significant gathering place that changed many lives. Not unlike other movements before it, the Toronto Blessing was also rejected by some leaders from the movements which preceded it. The overall body of Christ was not united in their response to this blessing. Some Christians declared the movement to be a false and heretical movement. They criticized the weird manifestations as carnal as many people laughed uncontrollably and their bodies were shaking like rag dolls. At the same time many other believers opened their hearts and experienced a dramatic positive impact and shift in their lives. This movement caught on all around the world in various expressions, with churches altering their relationship with God. In other words, it dramatically changed how they did "church." For us, it began a relational transformation with God and others.

In the Fall of 1995, something strange happened at a meeting in our church. No one had taught us and we hadn't even heard of the Toronto revival. The presence of God started to fall upon people and they began to manifest

His presence. It wasn't the same for everyone, but some were overwhelmed with joy and began to laugh, others were flooded by love and began to cry, and others began to have their hands shake. As the pastor, I didn't know what to do. Some people objected while others said, "I feel so much of God's love and presence." I shared with my flock, "The devil doesn't make people more in love with Jesus. We need to test everything by its fruit." This is a much longer story, but the point is that the leadership was led to embrace this as a move of God. We believed that it was His Holy Spirit, so we pursued and welcomed this flow of His presence into our midst. At the time we had no clue that this decision would change our lives and direction in ministry forever. I want to reiterate that we had never been to Toronto. After Pastor Arlan Askew from the Westside Vineyard came and taught our church how to hear God's voice, we began to move in many of the gifts of the Spirit. We didn't fully understand them, but we had a gentle and humble attitude about everything. We simply agreed to test what we saw and heard with Scripture, and to not allow our experience to be more important than that of another person's. In other words, we chose to simply love each other.

We joked that we were a bunch of Baptists with new power tools!

It wasn't any easy time. When your small stream starts to flow into a large river, the river wins! This is how movements begin. However, as the waters converge, powerful currents you don't fully understand are changing things around you. As a young pastor, I didn't know exactly how to navigate the transition, and admittedly made some mistakes. At the same time, something very significant happened. We were no longer the same, and we were now a part of something God was doing around the world. Many people want to focus on the outward physical manifestations of this movement, but far more than strange behavior was happening. People were now getting healed regularly and we were learning how to hear and to know God in a far more personal way as our hearts were changed. I cannot fully explain it with mere words, but there was so much more life and power in what we were experiencing. Our spirits hungered for more. Our first relational transformation was with God. Intimacy, encounters, and experiences of love became a way of life. Our goal wasn't to hear Him, but to know Him. God revealed Himself so powerfully and dramatically, it altered completely how we related to Him.

How do we Receive More?

So how does one learn and receive more? The answer is to seek out those who have gone before and have learned through experience. We therefore fervently sought out events and conferences which were gathering places where Spirit-filled people shared their journeys. Consider, for example, the story of Wesley and Stacey Campbell who pastored a Plymouth Brethren church in Kelowna, Canada. Now the Spirit had been moving within their church body for nearly 10 years, just as He had later erupted on the scene in the Toronto revival and around the world. So at the conferences, with hundreds in attendance, the Campbell's frequently shared how God just took over and how they learned to conform and not quench the moving of the Spirit.

Another significant place this move was occurring was in Pasadena, California. A church called Harvest Rock Church had gone through a visitation similar to that of Toronto. First, Pastor Ché Ahn went to Toronto in a personal season of defeat and discouragement. In his book, "Into the Fire," Ché shares how his life and church were dramatically changed after going to Toronto. What happened was that they joined and expanded this movement of God.

Under the leadership of Ché and Sue Ahn, Harvest Rock Church began to have protracted meetings five days a week for nearly three years. They also hosted regular conferences and events to share and encourage the larger body of Christ, specifically those who wanted to learn more about this move of the Spirit and participate in what God was doing.

It was in 1996 that my wife Ann and I first went to a conference at the Mott Auditorium in Pasadena, California, where Harvest Rock Church was conducting these ongoing meetings. It felt like a breath of fresh air from our denominational meetings. It was so encouraging to see that what we were experiencing was touching people from all around the world. Many nations were represented, and the hunger of the people was visible. People would wait for hours, stand in long lines, and travel long distances to get prayer and receive an impartation of God's love and power. In these powerful meetings there were people from dozens of other countries, and they all wanted to know how to be a part of this move of God. As we went, we encountered God and His presence in a way that was unimaginable. In fact, it was like what the early church people in the Bible experienced. We had visions and prophetic words that were amazingly accurate and filled with revelation. Yes, there were manifestations, but we learned that these were only a part of the movement. We could see clearly that God was using these physical things to test the hearts of the people.

The Impact of Dr. C. Peter Wagner

It is important to say that God was moving uniquely with different groupings of people. Not everyone was united into one movement, but there were certain similarities and powerful connections that were emerging out of the moving of the Spirit. In 1998, I heard a speaker at a conference in Portland, Oregon. This man, Dr. C. Peter Wagner, was a former professor at Fuller Theological Seminary in Pasadena, California. His resume was impressive as Dr. Wagner was in the mission field from 1956 to 1971 in Bolivia, and taught at the seminary from 1971 to 2001. Following that he started the Wagner Leadership Institute (now Wagner University, under his spiritual son, Ché Ahn).

This was a very important stage in my journey, and the truth is, I had no idea how much his input was going to impact my life. He was teaching on the fivefold ministry, and in particular, how the roles of the apostles and prophets are intertwined and connected. It was a very fascinating concept and I inhaled the teaching. His material rocked my world because up to then conferences only taught about pastors. Secretly, this meant a lot to me. The reason was that when I went through the relational and spiritual transformation I described earlier, I started to write down what I believed that the Lord was saying to me personally. We call it journaling, but in essence it is not only my thoughts but what we believed God was speaking. The main reason for writing things down was to test and keep record of what we were hearing. The discipline of journaling has proven to be both faith and character building. In fact, practicing this has led me to hear more and more clearly.

Beyond the manifestations was a profound experience of hearing God personally and powerfully.

Things that I heard were confirmed by other people that didn't even know me. God was telling me I had an apostolic and prophetic call on my life. I will share this later in much greater detail. However, when Peter Wagner spoke, it confirmed things I was hearing personally for myself and for our ministry. To hear that God was spreading this around the world made my heart leap with joy.

Deciding to Agree with God About My Calling

Central to my apostolic call was a call to go to the nations of the world. This is no small thing. This calling was confirmed by many people as well as from the Lord. I didn't know where I was called, but I believe it took faith to agree with the Lord that He had in fact called me to go to foreign lands. Peter Wagner taught so clearly that the renewing of these fivefold offices in Ephesians 4:11 were being restored in the body of Christ; at least to the streams that were open to it. Now, after study and definition, Peter Wagner was declaring that an incredible move of God was happening. In 1999 he came out with a book entitled "Churchquake" and articulated this move as the "New Apostolic Reformation." Why? Because he believed that this reformation was as significant for the church as the Protestant Reformation of the 1500's.

The fact is, there is not one group or head of this movement. However the characteristics are so similar, that indeed it is a movement that has been growing extensively since that time. Earlier I mentioned that Ché and Sue Ahn were leading the regular meetings in 1995 and beyond. In 1996 after clear direction from the Lord, Harvest International Ministries was started as a network of like minded churches. Meanwhile there were other key leaders in this larger move that started networks as a response to God's call. In fact, leaders of six major apostolic networks have partnered together in what is known as "Revival Alliance." This came out of the desire to work together and honor one another in the midst of major growth around this global movement. Many of these apostolic networks have emerged in countries around the world.

Before I get too far, I want to go back to hearing Peter Wagner in 1999. It was then that I realized Ann and I could be part of a global movement and that God wanted to us be a part. Peter Wagner has shared that he struggled with possible names for the movement. In an article in Charisma Magazine on August 24, 2011, Peter wrote:

> *"If I was going to write about this phenomenal move of the Holy Spirit, I knew I had to give it a name. I tried 'Post-denominational' but soon dropped it because of the objections of many of my friends who were denominational executives. Then, in 1994, I tested 'New Apostolic Reformation.' 'Reformation' because the movement matched the Protestant Reformation in world impact; 'Apostolic' because of all the changes, the most radical one was apostolic governance...and, 'New,' because several churches and denominations already carried the name 'apostolic,' but they did not fit the NAR pattern."*

It is important to put this movement into context, so we can share our story in the midst of this larger move of God. This book is to help explain what the apostolic movement is, and what it looks like tangibly. Ann and I have played a small part in the symphony, but we have gotten to witness how God is moving and this global movement is maturing. In fact, we are now seeing glimpses of measurable transformation and sustainable changes in the world. This book is in part an auto-biographical journey as to how we came into the apostolic ministry full time, and at the same time is a practical guide to understanding what it looks like in action. The key is understanding the relational changes and shifts that the apostolic implies and encourages. Thus the title of the book, "RELATIONAL TRANSFORMATION,"

Perhaps you have sensed that you are different than a traditional pastor or leader, and you have sensed God calling you step into deeper waters? If so, then this book is for you. It is designed to inspire you to interpret what is happening in your heart and how that relates to the Hand of God in this season. In addition, you may have had an apostolic call, or one of the others of the fivefold, but you are unsure as to how it goes from being a calling to a tangible expression. What's more, you have a yearning for something more but don't know exactly what it means. This book will hopefully bring a lot of this together in your spirit and give you a practical road map on how to live it out. I also want to give a frame work for those that are newly a part of an apostolic church or ministry. In the pages ahead you will come to appreciate the amazing shift that is happening around the world and how you can be a part of this global movement. It is time to unlock your apostolic ministry!

2

MY APOSTOLIC JOURNEY

In the last chapter I referred to the call to the apostolic ministry on my life, but I didn't go into detail as to how that continued to grow and become a reality in my life. One of the main prophetic words I received, was that I was to go to the nations. Many people get similar words and often don't know what to do with them. The same was true for me, because even though I believed I was called to the nations, I had no idea how to make it happen. Early on I had the wrong concept of how this would take place, because I assumed it would be a dramatic supernatural experience like that of Saul of Tarsus. I've joked that I expected the heavens to open and I would hear angels singing, and suddenly the globe would appear before me highlighting a nation or two for me to go to. I prayed about it and waited on the Lord, but I had unknowingly over-spiritualized it. This is how it began. I was at a conference and I heard an apostle named Harold Eberle announce that he was leading a trip to Kenya. So, I asked him if I could go and He said, "Yes." It wasn't any more dramatic than that.

First Trip to Kenya in 1998

In 1998 we went to Kenya with a team of 15 people. Harold is an amazing teacher and the Kenyans enjoyed him very much. He started schools for children, mainly orphans. He set up training facilities for pastors and leaders.

Moreover, he allowed others on the team to teach. I will never forget this opportunity because when I taught for the first time, I literally felt something different happening as though a mantle had come upon me. Harold was insightful and filled with wisdom. He spoke to me afterward saying that he perceived that something special was happening in my life. Shortly after the meeting people came to me asking that I come and speak at their ministries. Harold was gracious, and as the opportunities came I was released to go minister. This had a great impact on my understanding of the true apostolic. Harold had no need to control me or be "the man of the hour." He could have stated that this was his realm and he didn't want to jeopardize relationships. Instead, he recognized my gifts and celebrated my calling, and was quick to release me from his program and agenda. Note that his response initiated another step into relational transformation.

The next meeting had really got my attention, as I was asked to speak at a youth convention with approximately 500 present. At many of the meetings I went to in our country, the speakers would simply ask the Holy Spirit to come with power. After teaching briefly, I simply followed that model, and was led to declare that the Holy Spirit will come and touch you. "Get ready to receive," I said. What happened was shocking to me as the Spirit came with such power that nearly all the people fell down simultaneously. It wasn't like dominoes, rather a deck of cards falling at the same time. To be honest I think it was for me to see, that God wanted me to know that something significant was happening.

In the following days, I led more meetings and I was very aware that God was doing something not only through me but in me. He showed me that it was an apostolic anointing. The written words in my journal had begun to have a new and dynamic expression. The feeling is actually very humbling since I came to realize that there is a place of awareness that it is God and not you. In simple terms, you are fully aware that the anointing is doing the work.

I rejoined Harold and the team, and I saw the power and influence that an apostle can have. The people respected and trusted Harold and opened their hearts to him. They were sure that they had a leader who was interested in their needs. For me personally, I learned what it was like to step toward my purpose and destiny in life. In I John chapter 2:27, it says that "the anointing will teach you." This verse became a reality for me, something I could see tangibly and know that it was God releasing it.

Becoming an apostle was not my goal, but rather that I follow the Lord in what He had entrusted in fulfilling my life for His purpose. The call on Jeremiah's life became my example. In Jeremiah chapter one we witness how Jeremiah was called and how he initially responded. Immediately after God told him that he was called to be a prophet to the nations, Jeremiah disqualified himself from his own mind as he was listening to culture of his generation. The messages that we, His children, receive all our lives often tell us who or what we cannot become or achieve. Jeremiah thought he was too young and didn't speak well. I viewed myself in a traditional way, and it was overwhelming when I sensed God had something much greater for me.

The reality is that most people measure themselves by who and what they are told by this world (contrary to what God clearly says in Romans 12:2). Instead of obeying God, Jeremiah initially could not believe what God told him. Perhaps more powerful than the call to be a prophet were the personal words that God gave when He said that He knew him even before he was formed, that even before he was born he was set apart. I chose to believe and apply this passage for my own life. It became a bedrock, my personal faith passage whereas to believe that God had spoken into the womb of my mother and that He was steadfast in fulfilling this word for my life. I believe that I was called to be an apostle, but not unlike Jeremiah I did not know how it was going to happen. That's the way He operates. Some critics say it is prideful to say that is their call, perhaps that is why Jeremiah responded the way he did. Maybe he thought it was humble to say I'm too young and don't know how to speak. Most likely though, I believe it was a lack of faith and he couldn't understand the value that God put on his call. I am so thankful that God knows.

It Takes Faith to Believe God's Call

It takes courage and faith to fully believe God. The Lord clearly told me it was important to believe Him and to do what He says. This is what is involved relative to the call on your life; you first hear and then believe God as He speaks to your heart. Yes, that involves getting confirmation from others and the scriptures as well, but the foundational principle is that we must surrender our will and formulate a bond with God and accept His intended purpose for our lives. This may differ from person to person. I affirm that the Bible bears witness to this transition as we read about how Jesus entered public ministry at age 30. He knew the will of His Father to the letter. Scripture tells us that the first thing The Father had Jesus do was to be baptized by John. The Lord even confirmed His pleasure with an audible voice from above. This tells you something very important about Jesus and His obedience to His call. His purpose was to obey and to please The Father, but also the importance of recognizing the anointing on other people's lives. In this case, Jesus respected and honored the call and anointing on John the Baptist.

When Jesus went to John for baptism, the immediate response of John was to say he was unworthy of the task, but instead that Jesus should instead baptize him. Notice the natural response of John, as it was very similar to Jeremiah's. When we look at ourselves and others with natural eyes, it is easy to discount and even deny what God is saying. In the waters of baptism, Jesus was affirmed by the Father for His obedience, but most importantly His value to Himself. Many leaders struggle with this concept for we must understand our value to the Lord in order to understand our call. Remember it was before Jesus did any of the ministry that the father declared over him, "You are my son, whom I love and in whom I am well pleased." This is a relational transformation for any person to come into their destiny. We must believe and obey the Lord as we discover his purpose for us.

The Power of a Love Encounter

At this point I want to share a love encounter that really changed my life. I was a student at Westmont College in Santa Barbara, California. It was my senior year and I was a resident assistant at a dorm. Even though I was a young Christian, and had potential for leadership, I was struggling with sin. I need not go into detail, but it had to do with having a godly relationships versus worldly ones. At the school I had Christian friends with whom I prayed and lived a life for God. However, at work I met a non-believing woman and became involved with her. One evening I stayed out all night. Meanwhile, a Christian girl had been waiting in the lobby for me to come home. When I arrived in the morning, she confronted me and asked where I had been. I had to tell her the truth, and I felt ashamed. I went into my dorm room and begin to pray. I knew that I had a problem and that I was living a double life. Down deep inside it was not what I wanted. As I prayed I was very frustrated. I knew that Jesus had never sinned, even though he was tempted in every way. I'm not sure what my logic was, but somehow that made me mad at God. I said to Him, "You never failed, You never sinned, You don't know what it feels like to sin." Suddenly in my mind's eye I had a vivid vision, and I saw Jesus hanging on the cross. I could see Jesus' face and He was wearing a crown of thorns. He was suffering and I saw that there was agony and pain on his face. Then He directed His eyes toward mine, and they radiated with love and grace. Next I could see a tear blended with the blood from His brow going down His face. As it fell off his cheek it landed on to my cheek. Then I heard this: "While on the cross I felt your sin. I felt your pain and the consequences of sin when I died for you." Something broke and changed within me on that day, and I have never been the same since. All the talk about the love of God became a reality in my heart. From that day forward I've never questioned whether God loves me or not. Talk about a relational transformation, I knew in my heart that God really loves me and it is continued to increase over the years.

I've shared this vulnerable story to establish how God's love turned me around. Without knowing the love of God, it is impossible to come into your destiny. For me, becoming an apostle was not the ultimate goal, but it is learning to be a son who knows he is loved and walks and talks daily with the Father. Often, when I'm teaching on the fivefold ministry, I ask people to give me all of their titles for the day. Sometimes I pretend we're taking an offering of their titles and I tell them they will get them back when we're through...if they want them. Immediately, I tell them that the first title they get back is son or daughter, and the second is brother or sister. When we seek to fulfill our call that God has for us, it takes more than faith. It takes an anointing and the ability to receive the love of God that we so desperately need. In turn that's how we are able to give to others.

I believe it is very significant that Jesus was led out into the desert immediately after His baptism. You see,

He was different now, the anointing had come upon Him for His public ministry. So why go to the desert first, why was that important? The answer is that the anointing is always tested. Jesus fasted for 40 days and was tempted three times by the evil one. He resisted His adversary and was comforted by angels as testing takes a toll on the physical body. My trials and testing took place in a local church that I was serving. I shared in a previous chapter how the church we led moved into the things of the Spirit and the prophetic. It became obvious that not all of the church membership was excited about the changes. Nearly a third of the people opposed me and wanted me to leave the church. In many ways I wanted to leave, and even got an offer for a much bigger church on the California Coast. Yet, God told me to stay, but it was very difficult as all trials are. In hindsight, I understand why the people were against me and I can see their point of view. They had built their church with their own hands and finances, and I came along and proceeded to lead their church in a totally different direction. But worse, I was defensive and unwilling to love those that opposed me. I had to make another relational change, to love everyone even if they hated me. This challenge transformed me into a new kind of leader. It enabled me to value the viewpoints and needs of others.

Before I share my stories about the apostolic ministry, it is important to establish this foundation. Rushing to look at the apostolic alone misses the whole progression of how God births His character and purpose in us. The key is that it's the journey, not the destination. That is what the desert is all about, and that was true for Christ, for Jesus says He was tempted and kept His eyes on the Father and was determined to obey His will. That is what God wants for all of us, because our purpose is found in Him. It's not separate from His will and destiny that He set aside for us. Relational transformation is founded in love.

From the Desert to Nazareth

From the desert, Jesus headed straight toward Nazareth, the place of his upbringing. On a recent trip to Israel, we visited a site which is called the Nazareth Village in the region of Galilee. They told us that in Jesus' day it had around 200 residents.

En route to the village, Jesus had begun doing miracles all throughout Galilee. They had heard about what He was doing, and they were looking forward to seeing Him personally. In Luke chapter four we are told that Jesus went to the synagogue on the Sabbath and He was handed the scroll of Isaiah. In Luke 4:17, we are told that Jesus found the place that he was to read from. I believe this is very strategic and important for us to understand as we look at fulfilling our destiny. Jesus chose Isaiah 61 to tell the people of Nazareth who He was. He was the fulfillment of a prophesy given over 700 years before about the One who was to be anointed as the Messiah.

Four out of the last five years I have had the privilege of leading mission trips to Israel with Dr. Ché Ahn and Brian Simmons. One of my favorite highlights was when I stood in the synagogue in that Nazareth village which was the site of Jesus' proclamation recorded in Luke chapter four. I believe that the waters of baptism were about receiving and knowing the love of the Father, and the desert was about relying on the Father and believing his word. Luke chapter four, however, is about facing the fear of man and the ability to declare one's destiny in the face of opposition. Jesus declared as He quoted the scriptures, "The Spirit of the sovereign Lord is on Me, because the Lord has anointed Me..." Before we look at what purpose Jesus said He was anointed for, I think it is important to look at what Jesus was saying by His selection of scripture. The emphasis is on the fact that the Spirit has come upon him in a way that was different from when they saw him last.

We know what happened at the baptism. The Spirit came upon Him like a dove.

My destiny doesn't start with my will, opinion, or needs. It originates from the Holy Spirit, and He knew me before I was formed and set me apart for a purpose. When I first read this, the Spirit showed me that this would be the key to my coming into my fullness. We all say we want to be like Jesus, and the primary way to do this is to follow His example. Then we look at the things that He proclaimed that He was anointed for. I am persuaded that we can see the fivefold ministry in this declaration. Granted, He doesn't mention them specifically by title, but the functions are clearly there. He says that He has been anointed to preach the good news to the poor. Now the Greek word for good news, or gospel, is *euangelion* which is the root for the English word "evangelism." Secondly, He was anointed to proclaim freedom for the captives, with an emphasis here of proclaiming, preaching and teaching truth which leads to freedom. That is why I believe this is the teaching anointing. Thirdly, He was anointed to release the recovery of sight to the blind, both physical and spiritual. In that spiritual realm, He was anointed to open the spiritual eyes of the people, which is the prophetic anointing. The forth anointing takes the form of setting the oppressed free, which is to bind the brokenhearted and heal their hearts. This is the main purpose of the pastoral anointing. And lastly, He says to proclaim the year of the Lord's favor, which is actually a specific declaration for the present day by Jesus. In other words it was an apostolic decree by Jesus, revealed when He said, "Today this scripture is fulfilled in your hearing."

I am convinced and hereby declare that Jesus embraced the fivefold over His life, emphasizing that He was anointed by the Holy Spirit for this purpose. It is noteworthy to mention that the people rejected Him in Nazareth because they knew Him as a natural human being. They considered His declaration as a self promotion and that His claim to deity was blasphemous. Consequently, they drove the masses to the edge of a cliff to kill Him, and we see a miracle as He supernaturally slips through the crowd unharmed.

Facing My Nazareth

Earlier I spoke of my desert and being despised by the church people, perhaps my Nazareth. About a third of our people not only disliked the emphasis on the supernatural, the prophetic, and the miracles, but they also disliked the idea that we could have the fivefold ministry and its offices in full operation within the body. It was somewhere in the year 1997 that my wife Ann got a very specific word about the division that was about to happen. The Lord was preparing us so that our hearts would be ready to respond when the time was right. It was spiritual warfare to the max. There were mockers in our midst saying things to the effect that we were now proclaiming that Ann was a prophet. It wasn't fun...no way. We were getting a taste of what life may have been like for the early church. Instead of facing lions, we were the subject of the gossip hot lines. Ann didn't call herself a prophet, they did and then used it against her. They did the same kind of things to me, twisting my words and using the Internet haters to spew their viewpoints. In the midst of this, God used it to heal me of a defensive spirit and heart. I am sure those who oppose the New Apostolic Reformation will attack me and this book. To this day when I read criticism on the Internet, I pray for those writing their attacks. They are my brothers and sisters in Christ. I love the body of Christ and want to honor every single part of it! Praise God, another step in relational transformation.

It turns out that God used the stress and pain of that season to bring us both to the next level of maturity as leaders. The Lord taught us how to love those who rejected us, and honestly I had to admit that previously I had loved my ministry more than the people. The Lord told me to repent publicly, and to go to those in private whom I had alienated. When Jesus told us the love our enemies, He meant it, and I had no idea what this entailed until I had to live it. I didn't know it then, but this was the greatest training for me to become an apostle. There were hard lessons I had to learn. I thought I had the right to defend myself and God (like he needed it!). Here's a thought: when Jesus told the people to love thy neighbor, they asked Him who is my neighbor? He proceeded to tell the story of The Good Samaritan. I wonder what He would have said if asked, "Who is my enemy?" My answer would be to first say who my enemy is not. It could be someone as close as a member of your own family...or church.

After two years of coming into unity with the church and prayerfully working through various barriers, I then embarked for Kenya as part of Harold's team. I know with assurance that all the trials were on-the-job training for shaping the fundamental foundation that I needed to go to the next level.

When I came home, I actually was frustrated with the attitude of my church. There was such a high level of hunger in Kenya, and I had seen a significant increase in the anointing during the Africa trip. Yet when I came home, it wasn't nearly as high. Though I did see some improvement, I wondered why it wasn't as powerful as it was in Kenya. There was more work to be done. Another step in relational transformation, learning how to motivate people that may not want to change. It starts with accepting them!

The next year I took my first team of 16 people to Kenya and Uganda, and it was on that trip that I began to witness the power of the apostolic anointing. The Spirit had told me to use the prophetic anointing to open the door to the apostolic. So when we pulled up in our minivan to a new town or village, this was what we emphasized. We taught people how to hear the voice of God for themselves, and how to raise up the prophetic in their midst. Meanwhile, the team was there to learn how to prophesy and move in healing, and God came in a major way.

A Lame Woman Walks!

It was the month of August in the year 1999; after touching down in Nairobi, Kenya we piled the team and all our luggage into a mini van and motored across the scenic countryside of Kenya. We could see Lake Victoria, the Rift Valley and Mount Kilimanjaro in the distance. After driving at a dangerous high speed, our driver reached our destination in eastern Uganda. Uganda, once dangerous for Christians was taking off and her doors were open to the gospel. Our van pulled into a small village near Tororo, close to the Uganda/Kenya border. We went to a small village church with around 80 people in attendance. As we were worshiping, a woman entered the church in the most unusual way. She was sliding on the ground using her elbows to move her. I was perplexed because she was not even using crutches but rather moving on the ground like a snake. Our team surrounded her and begin to pray for healing. None of us have ever seen the lame walk before, and we really didn't know what to think, but that is how God had trained us. He showed us to simply have humility and not act like we knew what we were doing. So we prayed and asked for direction, and we bound spirits of infirmity and disease, and asked the Holy Spirit to loosen healing to her legs. It is important to say here that it didn't happen right away, in fact we prayed for over a half hour. The young woman, Agnes, felt the faith to try and stand up. As she did her right leg grew very strong and she stood up off the ground. To my confusion her left leg didn't seem that different from when we began praying. I was being trained. I didn't understand why one leg would be totally transformed and the other hardly changed at all. So we prayed some more and I asked Agnes to ask the Lord about the other leg. She then proclaimed, "God told me, now you are off the ground for the first time in your life. Use a stick and your legs will grow strong." So we gave her a walking stick, and she glowed with such joy.

That experience was a life changer, because I realized that I was focused on the leg that was not healed. Somehow I was narrowly looking at one aspect while ignoring the amazing miracle that she was off the ground for the first time. I asked the Lord about it and He said, "Don't pray for healing, pray for people." This was really important to me because 2 Corinthians 12:12 says specifically, "I persevered in demonstrating among you the marks of a true apostle, including signs, wonders and miracles."

The next day we headed back to Kenya and, as scheduled, we stopped to conduct a meeting in a town called Nyahururu. As I got up to preach I heard the Lord say something that took me off balance. He said, "I am not preaching right now." My mind was going in a circle; we had done worship, now it was time to preach. That is how we've always done it. But Jesus said in John 5:19 that He only did what He saw the Father doing. So I asked the Lord, "What are You doing?" He said, "I'm healing a deaf left ear." By faith, I publicly repeated what I had just heard. Then a man came forward for prayer according to the declaration. I asked him how long his ear had been deaf, and he told me that he fell off a ladder seven years ago resulting in the injury. As I prayed for him and lifted up my hand, he flew back over five feet and landed on the ground. I didn't push him or use force and I marveled at the display of power. He gave praise to God and testified that his ear was totally healed. With renewed energy, the team broke up into small cells and prayed for many sick people. We witnessed healing of all kinds. On the way to our minivan, a woman came up to me holding a young child in her arms. She informed me that her son was born deaf and asked me to pray for him. The entire team had already gone to the van, and no one was around. I suddenly felt so inadequate in fear of the Lord. I surmised that my fears stemmed from the intensive expectations for her child's healing. For a brief moment I wondered what would happen if indeed he wasn't healed. But my mind countered and reminded me that I was called to be an apostle. I had not yet been commissioned yet but I was getting powerful training. I knew that this was an important event in the building of my foundation. I asked God to open the ears to hear, and as I clicked my fingers, the child turned his head quickly and began to cry. The mother began to celebrate with joy and declared that her son was healed. I want to say this honestly that one does not feel a prideful boast in this moment. Conversely, the emotion is one of awe, gratitude and amazement. Your mind doesn't totally understand as your heart is drawn to the Lord. You can't believe you get to participate with Jesus in carrying out His miracles.

The Beginning of an Apostolic Network

During this trip, I was also learning the importance of networking and what true apostolic influence actually is. While I have enjoyed ministering in Kenya, there is an ongoing problem. The competition and desperation for money is something that I have had to deal with and to continually grow and learn along the way. My point is that it is important to be cautious and discreet in making partners in foreign lands and to discern whom God is leading you to in fulfilling His work. God led me to the right man. On the second trip, which I headed up, we were invited to the coastal region above the city of Mombasa, in a town called Kilifi. The contact was Bishop Joseph, who had approximately 70 churches that he had started or were under his care. In addition to the Bishop, there was a group of young professional men who were working in schools or other small businesses. I cherish the day that I met a young man named Simon Karisa. To this day he is an amazing son, and in 2014 Simon was commissioned by Dr. Ché Ahn and me as an apostle. There will be much more about this in Chapter 6 where I discuss apostolic fathers and mothers. As we began interacting with our new friends, we were impressed with their hunger and receptive hearts. We initially conducted three days of meetings where we taught them about the love of God and what prophesy was. It was difficult at first because the concept of prophesy had often been rejected in Kenya, and Africa too for that matter, because of the association of prophesy with witchcraft. Witch doctors' words were mostly very negative and they would lay evil curses on the people. These false prophets would extort money or gifts in return for their prophesies. Conversely, when we came with words of love and encouragement, the folks became very receptive and excited about our ministry. They came to believe the words were from the one true God because they were accurate and given in the spirit of humility and love.

As we ministered in group settings, we noticed that all the believing women were wearing covers or bonnets on their heads. When asked why, they told us that they were told that the women had to wear these to confirm their salvation. As for women who did not wear them, they were considered unsaved. We observed that their ministry practice had many other legalistic rules based on revelations given to Bishop Joseph. Two memorable examples are: what foods to eat and on what days, or the number of times a person had to be immersed while baptized. There were other petty rules that were also not based on scripture and I knew that confrontation would eventually be necessary. The following year we were invited to return and I knew that God wanted me to address these things, but I wasn't sure how. It happened one morning as I was preparing for the day. I heard the Lord say, "Today I will show you what the apostolic anointing looks like." He then preceded to give me a message entitled "The Letter Kills, but the Spirit Gives Life," based upon 2 Corinthians 3:6. From a crude pulpit, I strove to bring this truth, that their man-made rules were actually suppressing the freedom of the Spirit within their very midst. The Lord had given me a list of more than ten things to address including the bonnets and the baptisms. Since the list was lengthy, I knew that it had to come off in a loving tone and not as a reprimand. As I spoke through my interpreter, the room grew very solemn. The room was filled to capacity with over 200 leaders and church members from the local area. Every head seemed to turn and all eyes focused in on the bishop as the teaching unfolded. Some folks would squirm and look to the ground, then look at me, then to the bishop to see his reaction. It took courage for me to step out in faith and I could not have done it by merely drawing on my own strength. I was a conduit for the Holy Spirit; in other words, He used me. Another wonderful lesson from God.

Getting back to the story...when I was done I sat down and a stillness came over the room. For what seemed like an eternity to me, the Bishop finally stood up and gave his response. He spoke in English so that I could hear and understand his every word. This is how I remember that deep, deliberate, solemn voice, "Today we have learned that we have many rules, but some of them are hurting us and binding us. The truth is that we want to be free, so today I am canceling every rule that is not found directly in scripture." I was amazed as I experienced and learned firsthand what it was like to step out in apostolic authority.

I understood then, and I am still learning, that it pleases our mighty God when His apostolic leaders bring "new wine" to His churches whether it be in a mud hut, a store front or a cathedral and regardless of where it is.

From that memorable day on, my relationship grew quickly with the entire denomination led by Bishop Joseph and his team. Over the next two years, we brought teams from Oregon and California and began to build the region numerically and spiritually. While working with other denominations, we found that the greatest need was for Bible schools and leadership training. During this season over 60 people from my local church and beyond went on trips with me to Kenya, Tanzania, and Uganda. One of our main themes was to emphasize and teach African Christians how to hear and know the voice of God and to prophesy and love without judgment or negativity. With the permission of a number of authors, and we put together what we called, "Bible School in a Box." We chose four school grade levels and assembled the material into packets. We distributed the packets in different towns and regions along the Kenyan Coast and to the south in Tanzania. We marveled at how quickly these little schools grew, and before long there were 13 new satellite Bible schools. Each successive year we brought material for four new classes leading up to a "Bible School Certificate of Ministry." Upon completion of all 12 classes, we would hold a graduation. In accordance with their culture, they killed the fatted calf...literally. These great celebrations had a powerful impact on the church. It transformed the manner in which they moved and prophesied, but most importantly, how they found freedom in the Spirit. It was during this season that the Bishop came to me and asked me who he thought his successor should be. With no hesitation, I told him that the aforementioned Simon, whose day job was as a schoolteacher in the sciences and was in his mid 30's, would be my choice. He told me he would pray about it but agreed that it was an excellent choice. Bishop Joseph never called me his apostle, but his display of admiration, honor, and respect positioned us together in a non-competitive cooperative partnership. He looked to me for guidance to help mold and shift the movement that he had begun. He told me that the most significant fruit to come from our influence in the schools was unity. Moreover, it was not only within his denomination, but with other churches in the region. This inspired us to start a new network called the Rock Creek Leadership Network. I use the word "network" specifically, because it was not a denomination in itself. This meant that leaders who were a part of any other denomination could become a part of the leadership network. Bishop Joseph became the main promoter as he testified that his denomination had nearly doubled in a very short time while working with us. While our work was not limited to this one group, I was learning a great deal about what the apostolic function was like. Simon was given the appointment to oversee the schools and he was up to the task. His labor resulted in a growth spurt as new churches were planted and experienced leaders stepped up and trained new leaders. By the year 2005 we had nearly 250 churches in the network, staffed with dedicated, qualified leaders coming up from diverse communities along the East African coast.

Applying the Fivefold Ministry

Here I was, just a local pastor for the Rock Creek Church up in Portland, Oregon with very limited resources. However, my elders latched on to the fivefold teaching and affirmed my apostolic calling. Several of these senior leaders joined me on the mission trips, as well as other members from my church. Many of those going who had been on a trip before would say to me, "There is something that comes on you during these trips in Kenya. It is like a mantle that puts you into a whole different level. It is amazing to watch." It was true, I felt such power and anointing and it was changing my life. Fortunately, I had language and understanding that came from the influences of Peter Wagner and Ché Ahn.

At the church, we were trying to learn what the fivefold meant in practical terms. We would try different things ranging from very effective to not effective at all. We were in it together, and the church was loving and patient as I endeavored to learn where this anointing was going. One of my first intentions was to raise up those with a pastoral anointing within our church. In other words, I was going about surrendering my position in the ministry. This was becoming evident when some people asked these pastoral leaders to perform weddings and also sought council in times of crisis. There we were, a Baptist church undergoing a major change and transformation.

Now our dear friends were also great partners and became our associate pastors. James and Lisa Bradburn were all in with the message of the fivefold. Ann and I had been going to Pasadena, California to attend conferences for over six years at the Mott auditorium. These were organized and led by Ché Ahn, the pastor of Harvest Rock Church. Several years before, they announced that they had formed a global network, called Harvest International Ministry which bears the abbreviation HIM. We attended meetings to learn how our church could join, and after a period of time we were led to join the network. As I said earlier, our network had grown substantially, but our limited resources did not enable us to do as much as we wanted.

My First HIM Trip to Africa

In 2005, Harvest International Ministry announced a planned trip to Africa. The advertised itinerary was not possible since there were no direct flights between the cities. Since flights were only a few days a week I discovered it would take over three days just to travel within the continent. When I let them know about the itinerary concerns I was shocked by their response. They asked me to lead the trip. I helped them adjust the trip itinerary for things such as timing and a few other factors that I was familiar with. Over 50 people signed up to go to Malawi and Mozambique with Heidi Baker and Ché Ahn. This is a large number for such a team. When we arrived, there were over 20,000 people, and it was so touching to see them receive the word as well as food for everyone. After about three days, they told me that another leader and I would conduct the services and ministry for the last day. I've never spoken to over 20,000 people before, and was humbled and blessed to have the opportunity. We saw many miracles including deaf ears and blind eyes opened. I knew in my heart that God was expanding my apostolic anointing. No one had called me an apostle, but I understood that I was chasing my calling with all of my heart. Most importantly, it was God who was faithful and leading the way.

When we arrived in Mozambique we saw the amazing work of Roland and Heidi Baker. They went to this nation known for its poverty and resistance to Christianity, and they were seeing amazing results in transformation. As I said, this was in 2005, and there was a significant impartation that happened in my life as a result of this trip. One of the most dramatic ministry events happened that week. Roland and Heidi have developed and raised up many local leaders, as well as others who come from nations around the world to be a part of their Iris team. At the time they had planted over 10,000 churches, and I'm sure the number is far more than that now. One of the ways they plant churches was through evangelism done on trucks, where a group of 20 to 30 people would load up sound equipment and a projector to show the Jesus film.

An Entire Village Comes to Christ

On that trip, I was given the privilege by Heidi of preaching the gospel after the showing of the film. This is how it happened. We were driving in a caravan to the designated village. A local man joined us in the cab of our truck to show us the way to his remote village. He had never been in a truck before, as he usually walked on the ground. He failed to spot a landmark tree which marked a turn to get to his village. We drove past the turn for nearly 2 hours and were lost. While on the road, I had a quick picture and a thought come to my mind. I clearly heard, "someone's right ear is going to be healed tonight." By this time these kind of thoughts were common to me, and I took them seriously. We finally arrived at the village. I was told that we had to ask the village chief if we could show the Jesus film to the people. I'll never forget when the truck driver returned and said, "He wanted $4.00 but I bargained it down to $2.00." Oh well, I guess he knew the culture! We set up a portable screen and generator. As I was viewing the film which was in their native tongue, I noticed that there were at least 700 people, most of whom had never seen a movie in their lifetime. They were in complete awe as the reels started turning.

About half an hour into the film, the projector broke, and the people became restless. I had been asked by Heidi to bring a gospel message to the community, and we came prepared with two different interpreters to translate into their language. I proceeded to share with them how much Jesus loved them and I said, "Jesus is here tonight." They started looking around for Him as they took me literally. They had just seen images of Jesus in the movie but they didn't see Him anywhere. A few people began to get frustrated and started yelling at me. The crowd picked it up.

I asked the interpreter what they were saying, and he said they were calling me a liar because they couldn't see Jesus anywhere. I quickly tried to explain that Jesus was there through His Holy Spirit, but that didn't seem to help the situation at all. Then the Spirit brought to my mind what He had revealed to me on the ride to the village. I declared, "I will show you that Jesus is here tonight, because He told me that someone with a deaf right ear was going to be healed tonight." The whole gathering behaved restlessly and was driven by a mocking attitude. One man came up to me when I announced that Jesus was healing a deaf right ear, but it wasn't like you would see at a church service, because he had the look of a contestant coming forward on a game show. He was a scoffer making fun at my expense. As I prayed a very short prayer, I simply asked God to come with His love and power and to heal the man. Suddenly his face changed, and a look of astonishment and surprise came over him. He shouted, "My ear, I can hear with my ear." The angry crowd grew more hostile and suspicious and said to the translator that it was an act of deception and that I had brought the man who had been healed with me to fool them. "Lord, help me... I need wisdom." Suddenly something came upon me and I felt a surge of boldness and faith. Concurrent with the feeling I heard this loud voice. "Alright now, to prove that Jesus is here and that He loves you, bring me ALL the deaf people from your village and we will pray for them to be healed."

As I heard the words I shook with enthusiasm as I realized the voice was mine. Once again I was His instrument. With that invitation, they brought seven people forward for prayer. The first was an older man wearing traditional tribal clothing. After praying for him in Jesus' name he too declared, "My ear is healed and I can hear." The crowd knew of this man's deafness, so upon his testimony, they pressed forward to see what would happen next. The next two were young girls around seven or eight years old. We prayed for them and using sign language and asked them to repeat what they heard into the microphone. As they repeated the word "mama" which was the word we used to test the healing, the people began to shout with joy. All seven people, previously deaf, were hearing within 20 minutes. I had never seen anything like it, because when I gave the opportunity for people to accept Christ, it seemed like over three-fourths of the people raised their hands for salvation. Numerically that amounts to over 500 people accepting Jesus. We invited everyone who was sick to come forward. The team moved in great power and many received healing and this caused even more to come to Christ for salvation. As things were wrapping up, I asked those who had received Christ to raise their hands and to me it looked like almost everyone in the village had done so. The following was huge. The village chief, wearing a Muslim hat, came forward and asked that I would pray with him and that he could accept Christ as his personal savior. What happened next showed me a glimpse of what revival looks like. The chief grabbed the microphone and announced, "Tonight we have seen that Jesus is here with us, and now lives within us as we have been told. We cannot keep Jesus to ourselves, so we need to share Him with the surrounding villages. Every one of you who accepted Christ today and wants to go with me, come tomorrow at 9:00 AM and we will go to the neighboring seven villages and tell them about Jesus." I sincerely believe that there was an impartation from apostles Roland and Heidi Baker, and it was a significant part of my coming into the next phase.

Ché Ahn Confirms My Call as an Apostle

I had seen Ché Ahn many times as a speaker while attending conferences, but I didn't know him personally. We had joined the HIM ministry in 2004 as a church and as pastors. One day, in Mozambique, he looked squarely at me and began to prophesy. He stated boldly and confidently, "Someday I am going to commission you as an apostle. You are going to do what you have been doing in Africa around the world building up networks and encouraging the body of Christ." I could literally feel the authority of his spoken words, and at that moment I knew the Lord was fulfilling what He was telling me He would do nearly 10 years before. As my denomination looked at me with skepticism because I was affirming the fivefold ministry and moving and miracles, I wondered how I was going to come into the role of training and equipping leaders. I was certain it was not going to happen within my denomination. I didn't hold this against them, and I do appreciate my heritage and roots. However, when God is doing this thing in our lives, we need to listen and not be bound by traditions and our limited experiences. Relational transformation is not always easy, but these transitions are essential to come into the next level of our calling.

It was less than a year later that Ché called me and told me that the current Executive Director of Harvest International Ministry was going to the East Coast to plant a new church. He said the Lord brought me to mind and asked me if I would consider the position. I was torn as I had pastored the same local church for over 14 years and we had all grown together in the Lord. However, I knew in my heart that I was called to train and equip leaders worldwide. That is my passion. Nothing brought me greater joy than being with leaders days at a time and sharing my heart and vision with them regarding fivefold ministry. I wasn't yet sure though if I was ready to leave the local church. When I prayed, the Lord said He wanted me to stay in the Portland area. I had asked Ché early in the process if I could remain in Portland, but he told me it was important to be with the entire team in Pasadena. One day I cried out to the Lord, "I don't understand You're saying yes to the role, but that I should stay in Portland. Which one is it? Please show me what You want me to do." I went downstairs to share my prayer and thoughts with Ann. It wasn't even 10 minutes after I had prayed that Ché called me on the phone and said, "I was just praying and the Lord said, 'Why can't Mark stay in Portland?' The Lord had showed him benefits for me staying in Portland while the past executive Minister transitioned out. So, the Lord had answered my prayer very specifically and I entered into an agreement with the church and Harvest International Ministry to be half time in each.

My Commissioning as an Apostle in 2006

Ché had chosen 25 men and women from around the world that he felt were making an impact on the nations. He informed me that he wanted Ann and me to be a part of the commissioning of apostles. Surprisingly, he said, "I would like to commission you in Portland if that church was willing." That would be a large and unusual step for a Baptist church to commission an apostle. At the next elders meeting, I brought it up and told them what Ché had said. I held my breath and said a quick silent prayer. It was immediately answered but I was still shocked by their response. Everyone of them were excited and eager to do it. They basically said that I had taught them and that they had witnessed my growth into the office of an apostle. Let me add here that my own inhibition had been hindering me in the process. Sometimes the greatest opposition to change are the things that are within ourselves. New wineskins do not come easy, but they must be in place to receive the new wine. The date was August of 2006. We all stood with some powerful apostolic leaders from numerous countries. Ché had asked Peter Wagner and Heidi Baker to be a part of the commissioning. As part of the ceremony, they poured oil over our heads and reminded us that this was not about a title, but the release to do what God had set apart for us. The Lord told me clearly to never give myself a title, so this event was vital for me to go to the next level. When someone is commissioned, it doesn't mean they have arrived, but rather that they have moved effectively in a specific realm as evidenced by the qualities and character of an apostle.

That night Heidi Baker had fallen on the floor (as she often does), but when we were finished with the commissioning, she didn't get up. She was out, not sleeping, but encountering the Lord and experiencing a powerful vision. The stage crew did know what to do, so they simply wrapped Heidi in the carpet and rolled her up inside and took her off the stage. The next day she was a speaker and she shared her vision. She saw a girl around 13 or 14 years old. The girl appeared uncoordinated, her clothes were too large, her body was thin and frail, and she walked clumsily right in front of Heidi. In the vision Heidi was thinking how awkward and unpleasant the girl looked, but suddenly she heard a voice saying, "Here comes my bride; isn't she beautiful?" Heidi thought to herself that the girl wasn't beautiful, but then the voice repeated the same thing, how beautiful and wonderful His bride was. Then in a glorious moment, the girl was transformed into a beautiful bride. She walked with confidence, her clothes fit perfectly, her body was filled out and strong, and she walked gracefully before her. Then she heard the same voice saying the same thing: "Here comes my bride; isn't she beautiful." At that moment Heidi understood that she was looking at the body of Christ with judgment and prejudice. She also believed the Lord was telling her He wanted her to see the church as He did. Sometimes people wonder if it is really necessary to commission apostles, especially when the titles can become a hindrance? Commissioning involves great faith, to see people and the church with the eyes of God. When we set people apart and commission them, we're telling them that we believe in their call, and we bear witness that the fruit in their lives is consistent with the office of apostle. It initiates a greater season in the life of the person being commissioned.

You can see this in scripture. In Acts chapter 13 we see the commissioning or setting apart of Barnabas and Paul. We have met them both many times, and now in chapter 14, they are called apostles and are moving in a new level of authority and influence.

When Ann and I were commissioned, we felt different. We knew that God was opening the door to do the things that He had promised. Being commissioned in our local church and at the global conference was a perfect combination for us. My associate, James Bradburn, and I coined the word "glocal" to describe the kind of hearts we believe we need to have. Of course it's the combination of the two words global and local, and this describes different expressions of the apostolic. That is why Jesus said to go to Jerusalem, Judea, Samaria, and the uttermost parts of the earth. I believe that we have different calls and different spheres. Most leaders of a local church should probably remain and also be sent out. No calling is exactly alike, and it is important that every apostle has a local connection and relationship. We believe that everyone is accountable to others, and we know that people who claim to be apostles and act like they are not accountable to others have hurt the movement.

Throughout this season my role in my local church was changing. Much of it came through the ability to pursue the dreams in my heart. One of the most amazing things about the fivefold ministry is that it doesn't mean that one person and their vision is more important than everyone else. At the same time God amazingly weaves us together. I like to compare Him as a conductor of an orchestra of which we are all parts. As the opportunities grew for me outside of the local church, it allowed for others to step in to roles of leadership. When I got invitations to go out, the Holy Spirit led me to simply close my eyes. If I saw the tide coming in, I would stay home. If I saw the tide going out, I knew it meant God was calling me out.

When I look back during this period, there were major areas of growth that impacted us all. First of all, there were the annual trips to Africa. Many people from all walks of life went on these trips. As we grew in number, the opportunities to preach, teach, and pray for the sick increased immensely. We would go out in pairs and try to touch as many churches as possible. On our teams, we have had teachers, policemen, housewives, electricians, computer engineers, and many other careers represented. This is exactly what Jesus did in Luke chapters 9 and 10 when he sent them out in pairs to do the ministry.

I like to tell the story of Joseph and Heather who went on several of our first trips. Joseph told me that he was there to support his wife and he didn't plan on doing much ministering. One Sunday morning I dropped them off at a location. As what happens in Kenya often, they had to go down the alley to the church which was hidden in the neighborhood. It looked like I was sending them into a dangerous situation, but they were actually safe and had local leaders with them. Joseph looked at me with disdain, saying, "How could you send me to a place like this?" When we picked them up with our van around three hours later, Joseph and Heather ran to the van. Joseph declared how amazing it was, because not only had Heather ministered, but he had gotten a word from the Lord for the people. He felt God's love for them and shared with a compassionate heart how much it meant to him. Wherever we went, the team members functioned in their fivefold gift and ministered in prophesy and healing. Most of them had never preached a message before in their life, but I shared with them how to turn testimony into a sermon, and encouraged them simply to try. Over and over again teams came back with mind-boggling reports. One time when my daughter was 14, the team came back and reported that a woman had been raised from the dead! The main point here is that everyone was playing an important part, and even though we have different roles, our unity and faith was used by God to impact thousands. As usual, we were the ones probably impacted the most.

Bringing this experience back home was not easy. Not that we didn't try, but we found that people were busy and had little free time to dedicate to the ministry. We also knew that these gifts are applied to every area of life, but is not an easy thing for the folks to transpose all these gifts into their lives. This is the primary reason that I wrote my first book—to help people get practical ideas on how to walk in their gifts and callings, with the ultimate goal of coming into their destiny. It is all about qualified leaders being willing to equip people. I am therefore dedicating a whole chapter on the topic of becoming master equippers.

My Amazing Wife, Ann

This journey is not simply my own of course. Ann and I have walked out this relational transformation together, and it has impacted our marriage, family, and friendships. While Ann functions primarily in the prophetic and pastoral anointings, she carries the heart of Jesus (the Apostle) as well as mine. She has been an integral part of the transitions and incredible breakthroughs over the years. She is an expert team builder and always seeks to include and train others. Her pursuit of God's heart for His people has often been the foundation that led to many of the changes you are about to discover in these following pages. I honor Ann deeply as not only my wife, but a powerful apostolic leader that releases the glory and presence of God. Her quest for intimacy and integrity have impacted me greatly, and I believe are central to how we have walked out this apostolic journey. Thank you, Ann, for reminding me that the relationships with God, family, and others are the context of transformation.

The Heartbeat of a True Apostle

There are many other lessons that we learned during this time, but I want to keep the goal of articulating the apostolic in the forefront. The next year in church was about learning how to "give away" the ministry properly. We can become so invested and have ownership in our ministry, that without knowing it we don't recognize the importance of others. I believe that true apostolic leaders have a heartbeat for those that they serve beside. I tell more of my story in the course of applying the principles of the apostolic to relational transformation, equipping, and spiritual parenting in the following chapters.

3

WHY USE THE WORD APOSTOLIC?

One might pose this question: why use the word "apostolic" if it causes confusion, apprehension, and division in the church? Language is powerful, and to be effective it seems logical to use other words and phrases that don't possess potential baggage. Today I fully understand and appreciate this concept. The majority of my seminary training was at the Northern Baptist Theological Seminary in Lombard, Illinois. It was there that I received a Masters of Divinity in Theological Studies with an emphasis in leadership.

At Northern, there was never any reference to the apostolic ministry for today. It was something we honored and respected as a special title for the twelve that Jesus chose for his earthly ministry. It simply was not a topic that was emphasized. I can say that we never actually focused on the words "apostle" or "apostolic."

It wasn't until the time that we began to listen to God for our lives that we learned how to prophesy over one another. In the mid nineties, that caused a significant shift in our lives. We hear the Spirit of God today and use the Bible, covenant relationships, and the Inner Witness to test all that is revealed. As I went to numerous conferences and renewal meetings in Portland and Grants Pass, Oregon, and also in Pasadena, a common theme emerged. Over and over again, people prophesied over me saying,

"You have an apostolic anointing...." I heard it repeatedly, probably over 20 times. Early on I would ask, "What does that mean to have an apostolic anointing?" Later in the decade the answer I frequently heard was, "I don't know!" The only specific answer somehow related to going forth to the nations.

It happens that this was not something I focused on much. But after hearing Peter Wagner in 1999, it came to the forefront of my mind and heart. I began to study the topic in the Scriptures and in the few books that were written at that time. In desperation I asked the Lord directly (I remember the date, it was June 24, 1999), "Are there apostles today?" His response came to me clearly and is recorded in my journal:

> *"Yes, and you are called to be one. Do not seek the title, but seek the function...an apostle is a person who has broad influence and authority in the spiritual realm. It relates to the expression, 'genuine authority,' and it is recognized by all. Do not try to slice it based on roles; base it upon spiritual authority given by Me and recognized by others. Do not try to overemphasize the apostolic nature of your ministry, but the prophetic. In time the apostolic will be released. Your church is fertile ground for training and growth. It will be a great blessing for you and for those beside you to discover the joys of My design and order."*

Believe God when He Speaks to You!

I share this because my pursuit of truth was genuine. I didn't want to just accept something because others were talking about it. My first response was that I was overwhelmed. I was called to be an apostle. Is that something that I could accept? What did I have to do? Looking back on it now, I realize that my faith to believe God more than tradition changed my life. I truly believe it is more humble to fully believe God than to downplay what He says. Jeremiah offered excuses. He couldn't believe God and even told Him that he was too young and didn't know how to speak. I, like Jeremiah, became confused and had many questions; it would have been easy to talk myself out of the whole thing back then.

I will share a lot of confirming experiences, but the most important place to start is with the Bible itself. In my book, "The Five Fingers of God," I write about the Biblical basis. Some of this here is repeated, but I have rewritten it with fresh understanding based on having moved in the apostolic for nearly 20 years. The words "apostles" and "apostolic" are key words in recognizing the plan of God, which is to transform the world through Christ and His body (His people).

Let the Bible Speak for Itself

For starters, let us see what the Bible says about roles and titles. In review, we see that there are numerous job descriptions in the Old Testament such as prophets, priests, kings, elders, and others. Note that in the New Testament the words "apostle" and "apostolic" are introduced. Forms of these two words appear 82 times. In contrast, the familiar words "pastor" and "pastoral" only appear two times. Where did the term apostle come from and why is it important?

In Luke 6:13, the report of how Jesus named the twelve is stated plainly, "When morning came, He called His disciples to Him and chose twelve of them, whom He also designated apostles."

The context is found in verse 12 and it tells us that Jesus went to the mountainside to pray. The reason I think this is so significant is that it shows us the journey of Jesus and the strategy from heaven He received from the Father. He was asking the Father what to do. The numbers of followers were growing and Jesus needed direction and strategy.

Why Did Jesus Choose the Word Apostle?

Pause for a moment, because this is important. Why did Jesus use this title? We can find no previous Old Testament reference or any history on the word. Suddenly the name and function Jesus declares is apostle! Why not evangelist as they were being sent out to preach? Why didn't He call them "rabbi" or "elder," two very proven and logical titles of the day? It is also noteworthy that He didn't even call them pastors or prophets. All of these titles seem more logical and would bring a seemingly better transition from the Old Testament to the New. So why did Jesus choose a "job description" that had never before been found in religious scripture or environment?

The significance of this is that Jesus is making a declaration of the model of leadership He chose and felt led for the planting of His church. He was intentionally building His church on a specific format of leadership and function. That is why Ephesians 2:20 declares that "the church is built on the foundation of the apostles and prophets." Using the analogy of a building, as we add and grow, we extend the foundation. Also, as we build in other cities, regions, and nations, we need to lay a foundation. Jesus is always in the foundation, and if that is true, so are the roles of the apostles and prophets.

Again, where did Jesus get the title? The lexicon of the Greco-Roman world proceeded Jesus, so we can assume it isn't something He made up. This makes His choice of it very important. Herodotus, who lived from 484-425 B.C., is often called the "Father of History." He was a prolific writer of the ancient world. In his first and fifth books he refers to both the larger function of the *apostolo*, a fleet or envoy, but also refers to an individual or small group as *apostolos*, which is often seen as an ambassador or a personal envoy. Of great significance is that these leaders were empowered to represent, but also they were sent with a purpose.

In addition to Herodotus the well known historian Josephus also uses the title *apostolos* to refer to an embassage, a leader who represented a nation for the purpose of establishing relationship and those who sent them. The role of an ambassador is not to speak for one's own position out of their personal authority, but entirely is based on being sent on behalf of another.

Jesus was choosing apostles, those that would carry the power and authority to represent the Kingdom of Heaven. In Luke 9:1-3 it says, "When Jesus had called the twelve together, "He gave them power and authority to drive out all demons and to cure diseases, and he sent them out to proclaim the Kingdom of God and to heal the sick." The correlation between sending out and representing the Kingdom of God is spelled out. He is demonstrating what the word "apostle" means to Him. He took a secular term that most accurately captured the purpose and role of these leaders.

This brings such a powerful light on the great commission when Jesus commanded the apostles to "make disciples of all nations." Did you catch that? Jesus is thinking in terms of those who have authority to impact and transform nations. What does that even mean, to make disciples of nations? When we understand the role of apostles, it makes sense. Apostles, *apostolos*, along with the *apostolo*, the envoy, are to bring transformation, healing, power, freedom, and salvation to the nations.

This is what Jesus was choosing when he went and

prayed on the mountainside. I imagine it went something like this: "Father, I want to do Your will with this growing ministry, what do I do?" As He prayed, the faces of men came to the eyes of His mind and heart. He knew each one in person. The Father told Him, "set them apart and train them. Call them apostles because they are going to represent You and Me to the entire world!"

Jesus Started a Global Movement

Wow, what an amazing prayer time. It is important that Jesus said in John 5:19, "The Son can do nothing by Himself, but He only does what He sees his Father doing." Again, I ask you, why would the Father initiate something that would apply to only 12 men? The answer is that the New Testament shows us so clearly the raising up of many apostles. Jesus was just starting his global movement, and it was led by apostles.

I am persuaded that anyone who dismisses the title apostle and role of the apostolic is denying the internal evidence in the Scriptures. Tradition is not our authority, the written Scriptures are. However, what do we do when the Scriptures differ from our traditions? Hopefully we will readjust our thinking. This was a major shift for me and when I opened my heart and eyes it led to understanding my destiny!

A Movement of Apostles, Not Pastors

For example, for most of the world, a model centered around "pastors" is the most common. However, Jesus didn't even use the title pastor. Within the Bible, there are only a few references to pastor or shepherding. When the Bible does refer to this, it is more in reference to the role of elders and overseers like when Paul tells them in Acts

20:28 to "Be shepherds of the church..." Note that it was the Apostle Paul who told them to do this. In fact, all the elders in the New Testament were appointed by the directive of the apostles. If you read the Bible and let it speak for itself, there is no evidence that suggests that the role or title of apostles was to cease. For example, in Revelation 2:2, Jesus commends the church of Ephesus for testing the apostles. All the original 12 apostles have died except John, so why would they be testing for apostles if the role was ending?

Let me share two more portions of Scripture that are extremely indicative of the importance of the apostolic. Before Jesus ascended into heaven in Acts 1, the apostles and disciples (followers of Jesus) are told in verse 4 to wait for the promised Holy Spirit. Then with an apostolic command, consistent with everything I shared to this point, Jesus commands them to go to Jerusalem, Judea, Samaria, and the uttermost parts of the earth. This is in Jesus' heart, making disciples of nations and going to the uttermost parts of the earth. The point is that Jesus Himself did not do that. He chose to limit Himself geographically because His strategy was to send His ambassadors to do it. He was forming a "sending out" movement of not only evangelists, but also apostles and that they would transform the world.

So in obedience, the apostles and disciples go into a certain upper room in Jerusalem. What is the first thing they do? At least what is the first thing recorded? They immediately seek to replace Judas Iscariot. They are led to choose between two candidate men and in Acts 1:24-25 they prayed, "Lord, you know everyone's heart. Show us which of these two You have chosen to take over this apostolic ministry." Really? The first concern is to address that someone needs to replace and take on the apostolic ministry. We must ask why it was such an immediate concern? The reason is clear. Jesus taught them the importance of the role of raising up apostles like He did with them. The apostolic mandate was such a part of their thinking and understanding that they took care of it right away.

The next text is found in I Corinthians 12 following the explanation of the nine spiritual gifts. In summary, Paul wrote in verse 27, "Now you are the body of Christ, and each one of you is a part of it." This was the larger declaration, that every part of the body is important. Demonstrating that this truth of value is established, He transitions to the big picture in verse 28: "And God has placed in the church first of all apostles, second prophets, third teachers, then miracles, then gifts of healing, of helping, of guidance, and of different kinds of tongues." Paul is showing clearly that there are different titles and functions in the church, and all are important and a vital part of it. Consider the following text... in the church, first of all apostles. The word first is literal to mean first in place, time or order. It is of primary importance, not in terms of value, but in terms of function. For those who want to deny the role of an apostle, what do you do with I Corinthians 12:28?

My encouragement is that you look for yourself in the Bible and see the amazing strategy from heaven that Jesus received and then implemented. You will find the teaching on apostles to be central to understanding the role of the church and its leadership. I am not about titles or thinking that the apostle is the most important, but I don't understand how anyone can dismiss this basic tenet on leadership so easily.

Going back to my story, I decided to believe the Scriptures and to study it with earnest. I believed that God was calling me to function as an apostle. It was never about a title. Moreover, the Spirit spoke to me and said, "Do not give yourself the title, but seek the function." That was my motivation: to pray, study, and learn. It was about growing into my destiny, and so I sincerely asked the Lord to teach me what that meant for my life. For me, it was about allowing the Bible to speak for itself. This is what led to my passion for the fivefold ministry. I am not focused on apostles alone, as I love and value all five offices listed in Ephesians 4:11. Verse 12 is also motivating where it says that anyone with a leadership role needs to be committed to equipping the people of God into their purpose. We will look at this more, but let this point be made, that apostles and the apostolic are foundational to following the model and example of Jesus and His earthly ministry and teaching.

4

THE APOSTOLIC RELEASES TRANSFORMATION

There are many words that are associated with the apostolic, but the word "transformation" is foremost for me. As stated in the last chapter, Jesus chose to call the original twelve "apostles" because they were sent out to represent and release the Kingdom. As a local church pastor for 24 years, it was always a goal to reach out to the surrounding community and to make a difference. However, it isn't always easy to make a lasting and sustainable impact. We would have amazing outreach events, but that did not mean that the community was dramatically changed. At our church, we reached out to meet new people and lead people to Christ. I have to admit, however, that our primary goal was church growth.

Since 1999, Ann and I have been leading trips to nations all over the world. For the first seven years our destination was East Africa, mainly Kenya. As with any missionary endeavor, the learning curve to impact the culture is steep. As the material needs have always been so desperate in many nations, it has been common for fellow brothers and sisters on the mission field to view Westerners as their primary source for subsidy. The competition for funding has led to a distrust and complicated game based around money. A pastor from the USA, for example, goes to Kenya and sees the need for training and assistance. The host leader in turn is eager to host a conference for an event and submits a budget 10 times the actual cost. While there is a conference provided, the host leaders use this money to support their families and pay debts. It is an accepted and encouraged practice as needy people do desperate things.

It took some time for me to understand and work through this process. It made me feel used and dishonored. It appeared to be all about money. It saddened and discouraged me. Even now on Facebook and other forums I get regular invitations from various nations to come and pay for a conference. The invitations are endless, as it is a traditional way that funding has come to many developing nations. This is the mindset and attitude and almost everyone is looking for a sponsor that will come and help them.

One time in Tanzania a man from one of our team members stayed a few extra days in Dar Es Salaam to teach. The pastor begged him for a computer, so the generous man, wanting to help, went to the store with the pastor and bought one. When they arrived at the home to set the computer up, he discovered that the pastor's home didn't have electricity! This illustrates how good-hearted people go and want to give, only to be ensnared in an old wine skin of dependency and even deceit. This is a simple example, but despite such a problem, many great things were accomplished in the Spirit. It was all a learning process and for me it was my training ground for the apostolic.

Transformation is Strategic

The goal of transformation is far more strategic and impacting than conducting meetings for a few days. I shared some stories on my journey of becoming an apostle, but this chapter focuses on the ultimate purpose and goal of transformation. It is my goal to link sustainable transformation with the word "apostolic."

When I became the Executive Director of Harvest International Ministry in 2006, my team brought with us a network of approximately 250 churches from Kenya into HIM. These churches were primarily under the leadership of Bishop Simon Karisa along the coastal region. I found Simon to be faithful with finances and a great partner in building within the nation. As of this writing, the Summer of 2017, we now have over 3000 churches in Kenya, with regional leaders all over the nation. How did that happen? It came through an understanding of the apostolic and with major relational shifts that are in the following pages.

A Woman at the Well Encounter

In the Fall of 2013, something occurred that changed my life and ministry forever. This whole topic of transformation was weighing heavily on my mind. Stated simply, a good definition would be a tangible and measurable change in form and appearance. But what does transformation look like? What are the essential components? How can one know if transformation has occurred? The upcoming story will illustrate and address these questions.

Preceding our trip to Kenya in 2013, the town of Mtwapa on the Kenyan coast was heavily on my heart and mind. It is a town that has the allure of strip clubs and prostitution. Tourists and Kenyans come to this "sin city" for sexual encounters. This pattern has increased immensely over the past five years. Having been on the coast since 1999, I was shocked at how visible and blatant prostitution had become. Even during the daylight hours, the streets are lined with women looking for customers. The hotels are full of older Western men and women who hire prostitutes to stay with them for a week or two. The beaches are lined with women waiting for prospective customers. To add to this horror, young boys and girls are brought into the brothels by their families.

As I prayed about Mtwapa, I asked the Ministerial Association of Pastors if we could have a transformation conference through my spiritual son, Simon. In my message, I conveyed that we would like to have a conference that addressed in part the growing sex tourism and how we could be used to transform the city.

The response was unexpected and disturbing. The church leaders had no interest in this topic for several reasons. They viewed the prostitutes as a curse to the city, and that any church that took them in would therefore be cursed. Moreover, the pastors felt that if you allowed a prostitute into their church that the temptation for lust would be too great for others in the congregation. To underscore their scorn, the leaders claimed that some of the street workers were not even from their region but that they had come to ruin the town of Mtwapa.

When the team arrived for the conference, which was still being called a "Transformation Conference," we were discouraged to even bring up this issue. After the first day of teaching, I felt empty inside. I cried out to the Lord and asked for strategy and wisdom. In my prayer I asked the Lord for a significant breakthrough. I might note here that in January of 2013 I had asked the Holy Spirit to teach me about transformation. In fact the Spirit told me to ask if I could become an expert on the subject. On that January night I literally pleaded with the Lord for direction. Getting back to the story...as I lay in bed there were tears in my eyes. My heart welled with compassion for the street workers. Turns out that on that same night there was a beach party in front of my hotel. It went on for hours, and it was so loud that I couldn't sleep. Finally, at around 2 a.m. I strolled down to the beach to ask what time the party was going to end, and they told me 4:30 a.m.! I was not happy to say the least.

As I headed back to the stairs leading up to the hotel, a

young lady around 23 years old approached me. She was wearing a bathing suit top and very tight shorts, and she asked me directly, "Would you like a companion tonight?" As I looked at her something happened in the Spirit that was overwhelming. Suddenly the face of my natural daughter (Loraina, who was 25 at the time) was superimposed onto the face of the young prostitute. Even before I said a word, the young woman was taken back because she saw the look of fatherly love on my face. I felt it so strongly and knew exactly what the Spirit was saying. I said to her, "I could never be with you that way, I see you like a daughter." She now had tears forming in her eyes, "Me, a daughter." Both of us were being touched and transformed. The Spirit was at work.

I then told her, "The truth is this, that your Heavenly Father loves you and He is reaching out to you right now." As she looked at me stunned, I asked her, "If your Heavenly Father told me something about His love for you, would you like me to share it with you?" With eagerness she said, "Yes!" All of a sudden I saw the face of a young man and an inner voice said, "17." I have learned to wait on the Holy Spirit and as I leaned in to hear, I heard, "She has a 17-year-old brother, tell her that I love her like she loves him."

I first asked her, "Do you have a 17-year-old brother?" This is where you hope and pray you are hearing right. She said with amazement, "Yes, did God tell you that?" I replied, "He told me that He loves you like you love your brother." She began to cry, and she stammered, "My brother is the most important person in my life. I love him and call him often, and send money to help him when I can." As she said it, the comparison was hitting home.

Then I saw something in my mind's eye. She was now a six year old girl and in a class room of students. After the teacher and all the students left, she proceeded to go in front of the class room pretending to be the teacher. I knew then that she had always wanted to be a school teacher. God was now speaking to her dreams and destiny. So I shared the vision with her, and she put her hand on her heart and said, "I did that all the time while growing up, I have always wanted to be a school teacher."

As we shared about the love of God and how to follow Jesus, she felt overwhelmed by God's love and acceptance. She said she had believed in Jesus, but she knew now she was not welcome in any church. Many in the Kenyan churches teach that you become "unsaved" and are backslidden if you sin. I encouraged her gently to follow Jesus and to leave and pursue her real dream of becoming a teacher. She wanted to pray and ask for forgiveness and direction from the Lord. It was very late, but I noticed that there were over 15 women standing under the balcony of the hotel waiting for a customer. I told her that since it was getting late I could come back and share more with her.

The next evening I brought another team member with me, and as we walked onto the beach, a large group of the women came running up to us and said, "We want a word from God too!" We prayed and ministered to the women, including the young woman from the night before. However, after we shared God's love, we didn't know what else to do. My wife, Ann, was teaching on inner healing at the conference, but few were trained and I knew we couldn't minister to all of them in that way in the short time we were there. I wasn't sure how to proceed. However, I knew that night we had to do something.

Fortunately, some of my team members had the idea to ask them, "When do you stop working at night?" They told them around 6 a.m. So they told them to gather everyone who wanted to meet for Bible study and prayer to come in the morning. For a number of days, street workers from the hotels, including these women came. A church was started that week and it is still running to this day. It is shepherded by a long time friend and pastor in HIM, Mirap Osao. It is called the "Church Without Walls."

Loving the Street Workers Changed My Life and Ministry

A number of months before at an HIM conference, a man named Ralph came to me and said, "I would like to talk to you about a program I am doing in Kenya." He had been referred to me by other leaders, and they told him I had been going to Kenya for years. I asked him where in Kenya and he told me along the coast. Then I asked him, "Where specifically on the Coast?" He replied, "Mtwapa." It was the very town God had put on my heart. He was working with Christopher, a pastor I had met and ministered with over 10 years before.

When we arrived in Kenya, we learned of the program and the work they were doing to train the street workers as they transitioned off the street. We asked if we could meet with some of the women further to get to know the needs of the population. As a result, our team of 19 people met with the women in pairs over dinner in a restaurant. We asked them to share their stories and to tell us about the struggles they were facing. All the women were active on the street, and they told us the only reason was to provide for their families. Every one of them was supporting children, spouses, or parents. The women shared how they had been cheated by bosses, sexually abused, and were desperate to make a living.

After everyone paired up there was a woman in her mid 30's that remained behind to meet with me. She was the woman that gathered and brought all the other women to meet with us. I will leave her name anonymous, as her children and family did not know what she was doing. As we met I felt the Holy Spirit say, "She is called to be a mother in this city, and I will use her mightily to be an example to many." I shared this word of encouragement and it meant a lot to her. She told me that many of the young girls came to her with their problems and their hurts.

Suddenly, I asked her if she wanted to come the next day to the mini-conference where Ann would be training people how to do inner healing. I told her this would help her heal the hearts of the ladies that came to her. She seemed surprised that I asked her to come. I didn't realize at the time how counter culture this was, as the religious leaders would not invite them to come and learn how to minister. Looking back, I did skip a few steps, didn't I? Yet, I wanted to invite her to a new life of freedom.

The next day she went, and as she was being trained, Ann and her team were leading all of the people through prayers for healing and forgiveness. The woman dedicated her life to the Lord, and with the help of others like Ralph and Christopher, she left the streets for good. She indeed has gone on to start several businesses and I believe she will become a "mother to the city."

So here we were, into our third and final day of the conference on transformation. I had shared all the teachings on the apostolic about changing the world, and how God is using people on 7 mountains of influence to do this (much more on this in the next chapter). I then had a sneaky idea from the Lord. I asked them, "Would you like to hear a modern day woman at the well story?" Of course they did and now you have heard it too.

I shared the story of the encounter on the beach with the young prostitute, and how it led to praying with more of the ladies. I continued to tell about the beach prayer meetings early in the morning and about the dinner that we had with the street workers. You could hear a pin drop.

When I finished I heard the Holy Spirit say, "Be quiet and pray." Before long, the men and women representing over 50 churches in Mtwapa came forward and began to repent. They were crying and some prayed into the microphone, "Forgive us Lord for turning our backs on these sons and daughters." I will never forget these words which someone yelled, "Why did it take a foreigner for us to respond to this need?" It touched me deeply. I was getting a glimpse of the seeds of transformation.

From there it seemed as though a floodgate had opened. As hearts were softened, we took a huge step. A man who works with the Kenyan government Department of Health was asked by Simon to come and share with the pastors and leaders about the real situation on the coast. A government leader with a huge pastoral heart, Evans, ran the HIV center and had contact with much of the population. He stated that there were over 10,000 street workers along the Kenyan coast. This is remarkable because Mtwapa has only 50,000 people, so that's one in five. He was able to elaborate on the plight of the 8,000 young women and nearly 2,000 young men who were involved in the sex trade. He made it known how people got involved through corruption, deception, and desperation. After the meeting he kept on saying, "Where is CNN? This doesn't happen in Kenya." Even those who worked with Evans kept saying to him, what is happening can't be true, everyone knows that the churches do not want to have anything to do with these people. Evans was amazing because he has such a pastor's heart. He really felt deeply the struggle and anguish the people went through. I told him, "You may be one of the greatest pastors we have in the region." We are working closely with him now to reach out to the male prostitutes and are praying for strategy and revival among this people group.

The whole week culminated with a "Transformation Tea Party." We invited the pastors and the women to a hotel for tea. Numerically, we had over 60 pastors and street workers, as well as our team. We prayed and prophesied over each of the women and put necklaces around their necks as God's love was declared. Many wanted prayer and to confess, but there were others that just stared at us in unbelief.

Transformation starts with the heart of Jesus for the whole world. For years I had led teams to Kenya and many other nations. We had spearheaded numerous conferences, had started new churches and Bible schools, and had fed the poor and ministered to children. However, this felt very different. I like to say, "I loved the church, but the Bible says, For God so loved the world." God was teaching me about transformation and how to love those that religion rejects. I do love the church, but Jesus was sent to the world. I was becoming transformed. Relational transformation impacts how we view and impact the world around us.

Commissioning Our First Apostle, Simon Karisa

On the next trip in May of 2014, my apostle, Ché Ahn, went to Kenya for the first time. The primary purpose was to commission my spiritual son, Simon. When we arrived I was told that there had been great fruit with the women, and that a new church from the inner training class had been started. In our excitement they told us that over 80 women, mostly coming off the street, wanted to be baptized. We went down to an inlet of the Indian Ocean and Pastor Che, Ann, and I baptized them. We summoned the power of the Holy Spirit to come upon them, and many experienced deliverance and healing while in the water. As they came out of the water they grabbed onto us like fathers and mothers and we held onto them like our own children. It was another life changing experience. After the baptism, I walked up the road with a number of the women. They began to ask me, "What do we do now to feed our children, how are we going to survive?" It was heart wrenching. I realized at that moment we had to do something, but what? We did not have enough money to feed all these women and their families every day. I told them, "I can't take care for all of you, but I will try to bring more opportunities for you to get training to start businesses and for jobs." I made a commitment that day that altered our approach and focus for the region. This is what transformation entails. We are challenged to come up with new strategies and for wisdom on how to change a city or region.

The following day we had a meeting with the leaders of the community. During the first break a pastor came to me and said to me, "I am a little uncomfortable with the conference because there are so many prostitutes here." The women were so hungry and so unfamiliar with being accepted. However, what was most unique about this particular conference is that the young men were there. Homosexuality is against the law in Kenya, and is punishable. Sometimes the young men are tolerated because they attract foreign money to the region. Tolerance notwithstanding, it is common for these young men to receive beatings on a regular basis. In fact out of shame some are murdered. Evans said that while some groups want to work with the women of the street, no one wants to work with the boys. Yet there they were, listening to every word. God was at the helm.

A Deaf Muslim Comes into Our Meeting

God is so wise, He sent a sign to them that would bear witness that this was of Him. As we were praying for the sick, a young man with arm crutches came forward for prayer. I glanced outside for a moment and saw a Muslim man with a kufi hat on his head. There is some tension and there had been bombings and detonation of hand grenades in this region, so we hired armed security guards for safety at the meetings. I wondered what the man was doing as he glared into the meeting through the windows.

As the young man was healed, he threw down his crutches and walked across the room. Suddenly, the Muslim was escorted down the aisle toward me. He pointed at me, then the boy, then his ears, and then at me again. I got it right away; the boy was healed when I prayed, and the Muslim was deaf and wanted to hear. I just declared Jesus' love for this man, and then after prayer, the man began to repeat everything what I spoke. He said, "You are saying, 'Jesus loves me.'" He was now hearing! He proceeded to accept Jesus as his Lord and Savior. The people were rejoicing at the top of their lungs in song and shouting. One of the team members led an altar call and 55 more people accepted Christ, including 12 of the young men and boys that made a living on the street. God was confirming the gospel of the Kingdom with signs and wonders. Afterwards, people commented that they never saw a Muslim walk into a church and get saved. Equally as amazing, they had never seen these young men come out the hidden places and come forward to accept Christ! I just learned recently from Evans that two of those men are spreading the gospel to male street workers all up and down the coast. The next day we baptized over 50 more people, making it over 130 that week! The majority were men and women active in prostitution. In subsequent visits I was told that most have remained off the street.

In this chapter, my goal was to introduce and illustrate the impact that the apostolic can bring to a region to transform and usher in reformation. After going to a region for over 12 years, I realized that I had to be the one to change. Perhaps this is why Jesus chose the title "Apostle" in the first place. In the next chapter, we will expand on how transformation and reformation are released.

5

5 + 7 = TRANSFORMATION

If we have a heart to fulfill the Great Commission, it comes down to this...to disciple nations. That is quite a statement and challenge, but is this even possible? One deception of the past is that this amazing work happens primarily through a local church and its activities. We expect people to begin attending and in turn they will encounter change. As much as I love the local church, and believe it impacts people, it is the apostolic call that sends the church into the world that makes the difference.

When I was a local pastor, I never expected anyone to "disciple" a nation. I was happy if people filled the nursery or led a Bible study. I was trying to make disciples, but primarily through building the church. The problem with this vision is that it is too small, and quite bluntly, it isn't apostolic. I cover this in my book on the fivefold ministry.

However, what happened in Kenya showed me that trying to change the world through the ministry of the church was insufficient. Local churches are often insulated and even afraid of the world. In turn, the world doesn't like or respect the church. This is an over generalization, but something has to happen for the church to love the world. There you have it, "For God so loved the world..."

I repented for loving the church and not the world. In the last chapter I shared the story of the deaf Muslim that came forward for prayer and came to Christ. What happened after that was a new chapter initiated by God. God invited me beyond the church structure we had built. By the way, we had over 1,000 churches in our network at the time (April of 2014). However, we were not changing the world! Just because our churches grow and have numbers, it doesn't mean there is always a great impact on the community around the churches.

After praying for the Muslim man and others, I went to the altar and there was a note waiting on the pulpit. It simply said, "The governor's team is waiting for you." What did that even mean? How did he know about us? What did he want? Shortly after, I left our meeting with a business couple and headed to see what was up. What we found was a political team that wanted our help and input. They started by saying, "We have heard that you love our people and that you want to help them." Wow, that might have been the greatest compliment we have ever received. They proceeded to tell us their problem. They have tried to start businesses with men and women off the street, but they always seem to fail. Now with me was a man named Rick who possessed the skill of helping small businesses become bigger! Wendy, his wife, was there also and works as a real estate agent. The government leaders shared their hearts for the Kingdom and prayed that God would bless us with wisdom and strategy. They sought our help. The result was that we promised to start a business training school, which we did the next year. I will share this powerful story later in more detail.

Giving Away Our Ministry is Apostolic

At this point I want to emphasize that the topics of transformation and reformation are not only central to the apostolic, but are fundamental to the fulfillment of the Great Commission of Jesus in Matthew 28:18-20. Here we are told that Jesus said:

"All authority in heaven and on earth has been given to Me. Therefore go and make disciples of all nations, baptizing them in the name of the Father and of the Son and of the Holy Spirit, and teaching them to obey everything I have commanded you. And surely I am with you always, to the very end of the age."

The command starts with the authority of Jesus. This is important because it establishes the model of Jesus, that is, to give His authority to others. It started with verse 1 of Luke 9 where Jesus literally gave them power and authority to drive out all demons and to cure diseases. Then, in verse 2, He sent them out to proclaim the Kingdom of God and to heal the sick. Wow, he gave away power, that is the ability drive out demons and to cure diseases. Jesus also gave them authority, which is the legal right to move in this power and to proclaim the Kingdom of Heaven. This was not just for the 12, since we have Jesus sending out 70 more to do the same in Luke chapter 10.

The fact that Jesus gave away His authority is a key tenet of understanding how the Great Commission is activated. In John 16:7, Jesus said that it was better for Him to go away so that the Comforter would be sent. That is giving away your ministry! What kind of leader can say that? The essence of Jesus' model for leadership was to give away His ministry first to the apostles and then all of His disciples.

Over the years, one unfortunate failure of God's church was to not follow this example of giving away the ministry to others. When I was trained in seminary, the emphasis was not on how to show others how to minister. In contrast, it was about preparing us how to preach, to teach, to administrate, to pastor, and to govern the church. While we were encouraged to recruit and work with others, it was never stressed that our main task was to empower and equip others.

As a local church pastor, I found that most people expected me to do the lion's share of the ministering plus any associated tasks that may arise, as that is what I was being paid to do. There were some who wanted to volunteer at different levels to help in the operation of the church, but it was still my responsibility to lead the primary worship service, and to oversee the staff and the volunteers in order to carry out the basic programs. In my mind it was a privilege to have a full time position leading a local church. As the Senior Pastor I led most of the ministry and its functions.

When we began to experience a dramatic renewal and the shift that I shared in an earlier chapter, the attitude of being the minister began to change as well. A major component of this came as we participated in praying and prophesying over one another. In this process we caught a glimpse of the destiny that God had for each person. We always assumed that this existed, but it was never the main emphasis. Note here that the apostolic brings an entirely new mindset, and with it, new wineskins.

There began to be another significant change when we started looking at the fivefold ministry. It showed us how to look at different gifts as they were manifest in people's lives. The fivefold became like file drawers for us, showing as different personalities as they related to the burdens on people's hearts. I didn't really begin thinking this would be the approach we would have, but as we progressed, we found that God's design for the church was not a fad. Speaking with other experienced leaders, it became evident that the fivefold ministry was something that they had already done or at least knew about. Turns out that for us, it became a paradigm of understanding people's needs as well as their hope to make a difference in the world.

The Fivefold Ministry is Essential for Transformation

In this chapter, I want to look at how the fivefold relates to transformation. It is my belief that every person has received at least one if not two of the five spiritual gifts listed in Ephesians 4:11. The verse says, "It is He who gave some to be apostles, some to be prophets, some to be evangelists, some to be pastors and some to be teachers."

This describes the classic fivefold ministry and is often looked at from the perspective of a position or an office. I believe, however, that there must be a much broader perspective or approach. If you go back to Ephesians 4:7, it reads, "Now to each one of us grace has been given as Christ apportioned it."

Notice here it says, "Now to each one of us..." This is very similar to 1 Corinthians 12:7, which also says, "Now to each one of us..." But this refers to the manifestation of the Holy Spirit that is given for the common good. What is important to note is that there is a similar understanding given by Paul that these are being given to each one of us. While many people understand this in relation to the spiritual gifts of Romans 12, it is not been nearly as understood as it relates to the fivefold ministry.

Why is this so important? I believe it is the difference between a grace that is given in the manifestation. The Greek word for grace here, *charis*, can actually be translated "gift." The word is broader than that. In the Greek lexicon, it describes it as something that is given to bestow a benefit or favor. Perhaps more significant is the word "given," which denotes that this is something that we in fact possess or have in our character or being. We would be remiss if we skipped the word "apportioned," which states that there is a specific measurement that has been given to each one of us. This has become so inspiring to me, because I believe that everyone would want to know what that measurement is. Not only what, but how much? I believe that this refers to the fivefold ministry gifts listed in verse 11. The reason is that no-one begins with the full measure of their appointed fivefold gifting. We all have to grow and mature into the place where we could earn such a respected position. In my book, I use an illustration of five levels of each of the fivefold anointings.

Measurement of the fivefold gifts can vary greatly, from an individual operation all the way to the functioning within the office of one of the fivefold ministries. This makes verse 12 all the more relevant. This verse states that there is a purpose for the fivefold ministries, and that is to equip the saints. Suddenly the fivefold becomes the mechanism by which God uses to bring people into the full measure that they have been given stated in verse 7. In other words, He equips and releases others into their intended purpose.

Actually, this is very different than the manifestations given in I Corinthians 12. First of all, these gifts are given by the Holy Spirit. They are an expression of who the Holy Spirit is, and they are used for the common good. That is, to serve others according to their need and by the leading of the Spirit. This is a wonderful reality and something that is available for all believers in Christ who have received the Holy Spirit. Yet, when we go to Ephesians 4, we see that this is a measure given by Christ to build His church. To do this, Christ wants to establish five different offices or functions. Some people struggle with the titles, mainly due to the fact that they do not understand them. For example, most people would be comfortable with the title "Pastor," but of all of the fivefold ministries, it is actually the least mentioned in the entire New Testament. In addition, there was no one by name that is attributed to this particular title in the New Testament. This does not make this title unimportant, but it illustrates how very little understanding has been given to the entire fivefold as listed here and appointed by Jesus himself.

Since I have written an entire book on this topic, my goal here is simply to argue that we have ignored the five-fold as the primary design for God and His church. In this chapter I will do a quick review on each of the fivefold, but here the primary emphasis will be leading up to verse 12: "to equip His people for works of service, so that the body of Christ may be built up." This goes back to where we began in this chapter, that the goal and model of Jesus was to give His ministry away and equip the saints for works of service unto maturity. This is correctly and literally stated in verse 13 where it talks about unity in the faith and the knowledge of the Son of God. Wow, this is where I really get excited about the fivefold ministry. It is the means by which people are brought into maturity and the full measure of what Christ has given to them. This really sums up why the fivefold have become so dear to my heart. It has enabled me to understand that every believer is not only important, but is an integral part in God's design for His bride.

One of the primary questions I have received over the years of my ministry is about people seeking their destiny and purpose for their life. This is the essence of why I believe that each person should know the fivefold ministry gifts that they have, as well as the level to which Christ has measured them out. In some ways this may seem like a simplification, but then we should ask why we have made it so complicated. In this pursuit, I have never made it about titles or making some people more important then others. The whole goal is to help people discover what their destiny is. I think this is what people want to know.

So how do we know which of the fivefold anointings that we have? Earlier, I focused on the Ephesians 4:7 passage which states that there is the measure of grace that has been given to us. But this time I would like to give a brief summary of what each of these looks like. Again, the focus here is not on titles but rather on the function.

Therefore, people do have different measurements of each of these, and a blend of more than one is often seen.

An Overview of the Fivefold

I like to start with the pastoral, primarily because it is the most common to us, and then probably the most familiar in the body of Christ. I generally state that one-third of the Body of Christ has this anointing. This is obviously not a scientific measurement, but is commonly verified in the conferences that I have done among several nations. The pastoral anointing is about binding the brokenhearted, which could also be said that its main purpose is about healing and comforting troubled hearts. I know the other four anointings can do this to some degree, but those who are pastoral major in showing concern for others. The Greek word for pastor is *poimen*, and is also called shepherd in English. A true shepherd is very aware of and knows his sheep. When you're talking to someone, you can tell if they're listening to you and are focused on what you are saying, and if they are in tune to your feelings. Pastoral people love to listen and want to discern your real needs. This is why they're good about asking questions. Often they will ask you about your needs days, weeks or even months after the initial conversation. When in a church service or another group setting they notice who is there and who is missing, simply because they care about people and wanted to express it. I like to joke that pastoral people begin to pray for the characters in movies because they forget it's not real. It's simply because they are designed that way, to have empathy and to relate to people's problems in a deep and personal way. Many people have the pastoral anointing and are not called to be a pastor of a church. However, because they do care so profoundly, people open up to them quickly and seek them out in time of need. Those of the pastoral anointing have a desire to comfort and want to be there to support people during crucial times. Does this sound like you? Perhaps you have the pastoral anointing and you are not aware of it. But to possess this awareness gives you a focus for your life and gives you insight as to what you were created for. Just imagine if you became aware of this in a deeper way and began to pursue it with all your heart. It would change your life, and you'd be amazed how many open doors the Lord gives you to minister and encourage people.

The teaching anointing has a different focus. Teachers do have a love for people, but they believe that living in the truth with firm foundations is the key to life. So when they meet someone who is struggling, their initial response is not simply to comfort. Their anointing helps them discern if a person is being honest with himself, with God, and with others. Teachers don't like to pretend that everything is OK, and believe that sometimes the greatest way to care for people is to bring them into an encounter with truth. Sometimes this doesn't feel very good, but for the teaching anointing, the truth is what sets people free. Those with the teaching anointing treasure Biblical principles for Godly living, and they can communicate and motivate others to live out these principles effectively. Teachers help us to have a good root system because they instruct us how to be grounded and to be committed to the importance of what we say and do. Teachers love the Word of God and are always seeking for ways to apply it, both practically and tangibly. Sometimes, because of their love for truth, they can face injustice and dishonesty straight on. You don't have to stand in front of a classroom to have a teacher's anointing. Teachers need to be careful to not become judgmental, and to keep their hearts open to people even when they think they're wrong. Teachers are effective in protecting our hearts, and keeping us focused on the essential Kingdom truths that promote maturity. Does this sound like you? Again, this awareness could release and open up new avenues in your life.

The evangelistic anointing seems pretty straightforward, but it really is a very powerful and unique gifting. Every believer is supposed to have a love for the unsaved, but those with this anointing have a deep and profound burden that has been placed in their spirit by God. Evangelists have a genuine concern for those who do not know Jesus. In addition, they are blessed with a personality type that likes to meet new people and to be in the midst of varying situations. At the core is a deep love for the gospel, and an understanding that it is the very power and wisdom of God. Those with this gift have compassion for those who are living in sin, and believe firmly that all the person needs is to know and love Jesus. Not everyone feels the passion to share the gospel at any opportunity, but those who are evangelistic try not to miss any opportunity. They appreciate and respect relational evangelism, but do not ignore the importance of leading people to a decision for Christ and to ignite a love for Him. Those with the evangelistic anointing have often wept and prayed at length for a given person to come to Christ. At times those with this anointing can struggle with rejection because they are willing to place themselves on the line. Do you fit this description?

The prophetic anointing is much broader than just a love for prophecy although that is included. The primary passion of this anointing is to learn how to hear the voice of God for oneself and to teach others how to do the same. The goal is to receive directly from God in an intimate way through a variety of means and revelation by the Holy Spirit. Those with this anointing are eager to have visions, dreams, impressions, and pictures in their mind and or heart to reveal the love and character of God. With growth and maturity, the prophetic person encourages others through getting words of comfort, love and strength to those around them. Prophetic people believe that it is crucial to know what God is saying in a given situation, just as Jesus looked to the Father for everything He did. As with each of the anointings, there can be an increase in the realms of authority and responsibility. Just as Jesus taught that what we bind and loosen on earth shall be bound and loosened in heaven, prophetic people understand this concept in a profound way. Could you be a prophet? Imagine the impact you could have to encourage others through revelation and personal words.

There are many people with the apostolic anointing but they are not even aware of it. That is because most have never been taught on this important anointing. Those who are apostolic see the larger picture and how everyone can play a part. To the apostolic, working effectively and closely is essential for everyone to come into their destiny. The apostolic anointing focuses on how every person can be a part of God's plan in a specific and divine way. This is why the apostolic yearn for the unity of the body of Christ, simply because they understand that oneness and working together enables everyone to grow and mature as each member does its work. Those with this anointing long to promote maturity, accountability, and spiritual growth for everyone who is involved in the Body of Christ. Others typically do not recognize that the spiritual authority and influence that they have is actually an apostolic anointing at work. Those who are apostolic are often told that they have a fathering or a mothering heart, and that they have raised up their sons and daughters to be followers who want to model their behavior. Those who are apostolic are able to bring people from various groups together for one common purpose. These could be people that otherwise would not be connected as they are culturally diverse. The apostolic person has a passion for transformation and sustainable change that comes through working together and following the power of the Holy Spirit. As with all of the anointings, one can have a measure but not be called to the office. In other words, a person can be an apostolic person, and not be called to be an apostle. A strong apostle will be surrounded by those who have a similar heart and understanding and likewise feel connected and aligned with him or her. Apostolic leaders put a high premium on loyalty and commitment for the long term. Can you relate to this? God wants to use you to impact others and help them mature and fulfill all that Christ has for them.

When you read the "job descriptions" of these five anointings, it is possible to see some of each of them in yourself. So the question is more like this: which of these is your first and foremost response in most situations? Which one of these would you consider your primary passion if you had to choose it over and above one of the others? For example, I do enjoy teaching, leading evangelism crusades, and ministering to the needs of people in a pastoral way. However, my primary passion is to equip people for their destiny. People might say that they have a primary and secondary anointing, and this is a very important distinction to be aware of. In my life, the Lord told me to use my prophetic anointing to open the door to the apostolic anointing. In essence, He was showing me that my prophetic anointing was a step toward going into my true and primary anointing, which is the apostolic.

Primary and Secondary Anointings

I want to spend more time on this because it's something I just mentioned in passing in my first book, I think it is very important and will give people a greater focus for their lives and their purpose. The primary is your main passion and motivator. It doesn't mean you can't do other functions. For example, I can teach and evangelize. However, at the core of my being is the drive to help others mature into their purpose and calling (apostolic). You may have a core desire to be a comforter to the hurting (pastoral), help people understand and walk in foundational truths (teacher), to lead people into greater intimacy with God through visions, dreams, and revelation (prophetic), or to discern if someone knows Jesus and give them the opportunity to know him if they don't (evangelistic). Don't over think this. What really is at the center of your call and being? That reveals a blueprint of how God created you! Can you flow in other anointings? Yes, but I believe as you mature and define your call this insight will take you to a whole new level of effectiveness.

This is why you need to know the primary and secondary anointing, it gives definition and clarity to your call. For example, I want to be a part of discipling cities and nations. That takes a lot of faith to say, and it took a long time for it to come to that level. It is the continuation, or even convergence of my calling. The apostle Paul spoke clearly about his apostolic call. He knew who he was called to, the sphere of influence, and he pursued it with all his heart. It doesn't mean you aren't open to the Spirit to function in all five. However, when it comes to declaring your purpose, you will find it is much more powerful and fulfilling to focus on the major passions and desires the Lord has given to you.

Now, let's look at the secondary. This is a step toward defining your primary anointing. It gives further direction for how you express your primary. An analogy I use is a rifle, it has a sight close to your eye at the back, and then a sight at the front (or end) which you align with the back one. For example, I am apostolic primary, and prophetic secondary. This means that the major method or approach I utilize is to move in the prophetic. It opens the hearts and minds of the leaders and people that I am called to serve.

Let me give another example, let's say someone has a primary anointing of a teacher, but the secondary anointing will actually be a major way of explaining the focus of what the teacher deems important. If the teacher has a secondary anointing of the pastoral, they will tend to focus most on relationships, matters of the heart, inner healing, and comfort. If the teacher has a secondary anointing of the prophetic they will tend to focus most on training people in the prophetic. They will show people how to interpret dreams, how to discern if you are hearing God clearly, and how to test what you're hearing. You see the secondary anointing is the direction that the primary anointing points to. In addition, as in my situation, this secondary can open the door to the primary anointing.

There are many examples of this, Ché Ahn is an apostle-evangelist, he regularly gave an opportunity to accept Jesus at The Call events. At The Call Tennessee he took an alter call at an all day prayer event that had temperatures over 100 degrees. Who would come to pray all day as an unbeliever, right? Ché knew that people came to the region and brought their friends, family, and hosts. Hundreds of people accepted Christ. Bill Johnson is an apostle-teacher, and his teaching has reignited many to hunger to be a teacher based on revelation from the Spirit. This opened the door to his apostolic influence.

The goal here is to help you have faith for and least one and hopefully two of these anointings and to see them as a blueprint for your life. If this is of interest to you that I encourage you to read my book, "The Five Fingers of God." However, my hope here is that you will see for your own life that God has given you a measure and created a deeper desire to discover what that is. Virtually every person has asked, "What is my purpose and life?" And certainly the answer is much broader than the fivefold and can be approached from many angles, I believe that this can be very helpful for an individual to articulate based on the passion and the anointing that Christ has given them.

I want to put this in its proper place or setting. The truth is everyone can't serve full-time in the church. It is often said that 10% of the church does 90% of the work. Even if you're in a strong church that had 25% very active and serving, there is no way the entire church could be or even should be focused on the operations within the building or programs. In fact where do people spend most of their time? Certainly it isn't at the church but rather in their homes, workplaces, schools, and neighborhoods. Most people spend more time running errands or engaging in some form of entertainment then they do in attending or serving a church. This actually is that the foundation of why most people are not equipped. Traditional leaders and churches limit the equipping as it relates to serving at the church or in some church related ministry.

Outside of the church the themes of coaching and mentoring are very common, and in many workplaces training programs are very precise to reach specific goals. I believe that the fivefold ministry needs to go far beyond the local church and is related to every area and sphere of life. The reason is in each of the ministry carries a heartfelt burden and passion within each person. This is what makes our individuality and God's design of each of us so exciting. There are numerous ways to discover your destiny but I believe identifying and pursuing your primary and secondary anointings can lead to greater maturity.

The Seven Mountains Represent Spheres of Influence

With the five of "5 + 7 = Transformation" explained, what about the seven that is a part of our equation? The fivefold is about coming into your fullness and destiny, but over the years this has been too limited in its focus and breadth. The church has often been focused on itself and has limited the fivefold within the church walls. Even though the fivefold is raised up and nurtured, the fivefold relates to every area of life. What I mean is that the majority of our lives are spent outside of church activities. And when it comes to the fivefold, if we emphasize the functions, then we focus on how our particular anointing expresses itself practically. For example those with the pastoral gift tend to be more focused on giving comfort and encouraging people. While someone with the teaching gift now focuses more on how to live out the truth consistently. Our fivefold gift is directly related to how we interact with people and actually can reveal the primary focus of our lives. This takes place at home, at a coffee shop, in our work settings, as well as our main efforts within the church ministries. Much more about this later, but this represents the five in the equation.

What about the seven, what does that stand for? This is what is known as the "Seven Mountain Mandate." The seven mountain teaching is most commonly associated with two amazing teachers and prophets: Lance Wallnau and Johnny Enlow. Both acknowledge it did not originate with them, however they are the primary proponents of the teaching in recent history. The reality is that less than 1% of church attenders will be employed in a church or ministry. That means that 99% of the people will serve in the church or will find the majority of their lives spent in another realm beyond the church. These mountains represent different spheres or realms of authority that people function within.

Those who served in the church or a religious capacity are a part of the Religion Mountain. This is very recognizable to most people, because it includes those who are a part of a traditional church, a para-church ministry, a teaching school such as a seminary, or missionaries that focus primarily on church planting and training, or a variety of other roles such as chaplains and Bible counselors.

Over the years I think it is safe to say that the church

has been focused on itself and the impact it can make through religious activities. This is a part of the picture, and most churches do have a heart for the community and want to make an impact. However, when people decide to join a church, the focus is often on how to serve the church and to help it grow. People from all different spheres of society are coming and sitting in church pews. This is where the other six mountains come into play. Perhaps it would be helpful to list them here. They are the Family Mountain, the Education Mountain, the Business Mountain, the Government Mountain, the Media Mountain, and the Arts and Entertainment Mountain.

The Family Mountain focuses on the importance of the fundamental building block of any culture. The family unit is the primary instrument that God uses to teach us about what is important in life, how to love God as well as how to love others. The family is the ultimate discipleship arena, and plays the primary influence in one's development. This is why there has been so much attack by the enemy and why we need leaders in this area to strengthen, encourage, and protect our families. The family is actually in the news quite often as people try to redefine what a family is and is not.

The Education mountain focuses on the preparation and training of the generations to be productive in the world. The educational system was once mostly led by the family and the church. However, in the last century this has been transferred to public and private enterprises outside the influence of the home. This proliferation has led to many specializations related to age, topics, and skills. This mountain is considered a pillar to society and in some cultures the most important factor in people's minds. Education can have a great impact on forming world views, concepts of God, and defining personal identity. Certain institutions command great respect for their influence on society. This mountain has many roles ranging from teachers, administrators, planners and counselors, all of which can have a great impact on thinking and perceptions of truth.

The Business mountain focuses on developing strong and prosperous financial and commercial institutions that provide opportunities for people to attain a desirable quality of life. Effective and growing companies impact the community by providing jobs and careers. Creativity and prudent management are essential for establishing a company that sustains profit and has growth and expansion as goals. The range can be from small shops to large corporations that have a global reach. This mountain impacts the daily lives of every family and can impact an entire region. The way a business treats its employees and pours back into the community will have lasting influence. Unfortunately, as with each mountain, negative and illegal business ventures have the same ability to impact a region adversely. The importance of Godly business owners can not be understated.

The Government mountain may affect the practical lives of every person in measurable ways. Laws, law enforcement, and lack of these things directly establish boundaries and opportunities for those within the scope of the authority. Governmental bodies exist at the city, county, state, and national levels. Other governmental bodies such as park districts, home owners associations, and municipalities can literally make rules and guidelines that impact our freedoms and rights. We are called to submit to the government as they are appointed by God to establish order. Over the decades, Christians have often avoided the need to be involved as politicians, relegating it to those who are not concerned with biblical values or Kingdom principles. We need Godly people to seek offices of influence and jurisdiction to release the Kingdom values on this earth.

The Media mountain has a variety of expressions through television, newspapers, magazines, and more than all of these, the Internet. The motivation to impact and intentionally direct people's thinking and opinions are at the central purpose of these organizations. The media outlets attempt to impact all the other mountains aggressively, and in turn influence culture through clever advertising and sales pitches. This mountain has vehicles now to barrage every willing person with information and images. These are now available to audiences much younger then previous generations. The impact of the American media organizations has a global reach and alters the norms of many nations. The competing messages to push the limits of cultural taboos has infiltrated the minds and impacted the acceptance and laws of diverse groups.

The Arts and Entertainment mountain has grown widely in diversity with new methods of expression. Traditional forms of film, music, athletics, art, theater and dance have an incredible impact on culture. However, there are other newer forms through computers like gaming, adult entertainment, gambling, and sports leagues just to name a few. Only the imagination can limit the breadth of what people are now calling entertainment, and some of it is perverse and grotesque. On the other hand, the potential for positive impact and influence has increased as well. Those who are successful can gain amazing avenues of impact with having millions of followers on social media. This mountain has always provided role models and people of influence that is gained through popularity and achievement.

I took the time to describe these mountains to simply iterate the power to influence the lives of people on a daily basis. It is a basic summary and I encourage you to purchase and pursue other resources that explain this topic much further. For years, the church and its leaders have tried to impact through the religion mountain, only to be counted as irrelevant to the other mountains. As Paul wrote in Ephesians, "We do not fight against flesh and blood." The battle for our culture and generations is fought on the seven mountains. We now need churches that actively train and equip the participants how to influence the mountain on which they live and operate in their work and focus. Each mountain has peaks where people can climb into positions that can dramatically alter the environment to which they are sent.

The fivefold is closely related to this, because it will be related to what can be imparted and the methods to which the influence is sustained. A pastoral business leader is different from an apostolic business leader. In my church in Portland, Oregon, we had some powerful pastoral business leaders. One man and his wife so effectively pastored their business that when we went to a Promise Keepers meeting in Seattle in 1997, almost every man in his company of 40 men went with him!

To understand transformation, and then reformation, we must understand the spheres of influence that we have. The Apostle Paul wrote in 2 Corinthians 9:13, "We, however, will not boast beyond proper limits, but will confine our boasting to the sphere of service God himself has assigned to us, a sphere that also includes you." Note that Paul understands clearly his "sphere of service." This is the core principle that leads to transformation. Every believer, and every person for that matter, has a sphere of influence. Some of these are easy to measure by positions, ownership, titles, appointments, or assignments. Other ways are attained through relational influence, the ability to mobilize and organize people around ideas, and ultimately to impact the decisions and actions of others.

As I shared earlier, I looked to the religion mountain in Kenya to transform the culture. Ironically they had no desire or inclination to reach out to the prostitutes in fear that they would pollute and corrupt their churches. Ultimately, through relationships and building on the business mountain we have seen progress. This is an example of a relational transformation that was key to a break through. We have witnessed reformation as the number of prostitutes has gone down according to our Apostle Simon Karisa. Last time we were in Mtwapa in May of 2017 we went down the "strip" where many prostitutes had been visible in the past. However, this time there were virtually none on the street. I asked Simon where they were, and he replied, "You declared the glory of God was coming to our city, and it did!"

Personal Application

Now it comes down to you. To be a part of this equation, look at your fivefold anointings, then directly apply them to the mountain on which you are called to be an agent of change. Next, we need to seek the Lord to show us the sphere of influence we have and that He wants to give to us. As a follower of Jesus, you are now called to participate in discipling nations. The good news is that we don't need to do this by ourselves. We are a part of a body, a family, and a powerful army of people lovers. We love Jesus and those who are in the world. It is vital that everyone believes that the sphere and gifts they have are important, and especially to break away from the old thinking that the religious leaders are the most important. They do have one significant role, and that is to raise and equip others into their purpose and destiny.

PART II:

THE EXPRESSION OF RELATIONAL TRANSFORMATION

6

APOSTOLIC FATHERING AND MOTHERING

Due to the rise in divorce and the demise of families, there has been much attention given to the lack of fathers and mothers in nuclear American families. It isn't that single parents don't try (because they do, usually giving their all and in a sacrificial way), but having only one parent in a home or having split custody comes with a new set of challenges. This same challenge of missing fathers and mothers is also frequently articulated in the church; many people will tell you they have never felt discipled or mentored, let alone experienced the covenant relationship of a spiritual mother or father.

Looking back on my spiritual life, my natural parents did have a part in it. However, I didn't really start walking with Christ until after I left the home. My decision didn't happen within the context of a local church ministry. My immediate support came from friends who were also new Christians. Along the way there were people that did take some interest in me personally, but it was more sporadic as it related to events that involved the building of ongoing relationships. That is how most churches are set up, because it is impossible for everyone to relate to the pastor in a deep personal way.

This is one of the main problems I have with the title pastor as it sets us up for failure and disappointment. The title implies that this one man or woman will be the primary spiritual leader in our lives. What happens when the pastor isn't even pastoral? That is actually very common and leads people to a lot of disillusionment, and they will bemoan that the pastor doesn't even know their name. This expectation of a pastor is actually unhealthy and impossible to fulfill. For example, it isn't best for a male pastor in his late forties to spend a lot of time with the girl that is 12 years old. We also understand that in certain other situations it would be inappropriate for the male pastor to be the primary caregiver.

However, the need for a fathering and mothering is buried deep within us, and people place these expectations on leaders without realizing it. There was a season where I really enjoyed counseling and meeting with people to talk about their needs. Yet, the more experienced I became, I realized that it was not intermittent counseling that people needed, but rather consistent and loving leaders that could relate to the people and walk them through life's challenges. As I started to move into the apostolic, I sensed a shifting from out of the pastoral role that I was expected to play. It wasn't an intentional choice at first, but rather a recognition in my own spirit that I had to change and mature in how I related to people. When I began teaching on the fivefold ministry and recognized that the apostolic and prophetic anointings were there in my life, it became so freeing to me. I didn't have to feel guilty for the ways I didn't feel, and I could learn that what I had to give the people was unique and important as well. This became my impetus: to equip and raise up pastoral people in the church. In some ways this worked, as various caregiver roles were spread out throughout the congregation and shared by many. I realized that I had to give away my role as pastor to many people in my church. I trained over 25 people how to move in this anointing and publicly gave away the role in a worship service.

As I worked in churches during my seminary training, I can't say that I understood what it meant to be fathered. I did learn by watching. For example, I worked for my father-in-law, Melvin DeVries. He is a great man with a big evangelistic-pastoral heart. I learned from him, and he always challenged me to be focused on the needs of the people. He was and is a great example and mentor. That was a short period of fathering as I went off to Chicago for seminary.

However, as I worked in churches during my seminary training, I cannot say that anyone really fathered me in the context of which I served. As an intern, I was given a role and told what to do, but generally I was just given responsibility in the area of youth outreach. For the most part it wasn't very personal and the training was very informal, and more implied than direct. While serving in my first church, there was a retired pastor that worked part time visiting the sick and elderly. I sought him out for a season and he was a gentle man with great wisdom, but that too was more of a formality than a fathering relationship.

When I received my own church, I had hopes that the executive or regional ministers would play some kind of mentoring role. However, in my case during the first five years I might have seen this happen about once per year. I have found this to be quite common as I work with pastors; they feel very much on their own. Even though they might go to a conference or reach out to someone more experienced in a time of difficulty, it is more limited to being focused on the situation than on an ongoing relationship of support and parenting.

Our church in Portland Oregon began to change radically into the things of the spirit and apostolic. Moreover, the Regional minister had never visited our church for the past three years. The old guard within our church became whistle blowers. They contacted him when we started praying for healing, deliverance, and prophesy. To give them credit, we actually were kind of wild, like a Baptist running around with a whole new set of power tools! The response of this leader and his team was not to reach out and support us as pastors, but instead, a fear arose that they might lose the church. Never once did he ask me for my side or what we're going through, but instead he wanted to meet with me where he told me it was unethical for me to stay at the church. His reason was that I had taken the church in a totally different direction than what the original members had intended. He was right in part, but he neglected the fact that the church had doubled in size in a year's time, and that many of the new members were very joyful about what was happening. Believe me that if the Lord would release me to go, I would've been dancing with joy, but that is not what He had in store for me or for our church. My main point here is that instead of being fathered, I was being treated like I didn't belong. When it came down to it, I was not valued nor fathered.

Many Leaders Have an Orphan Heart

There is a great deal of teaching on the "orphan heart" or spirit. This is extremely relevant to the chapter at hand. Those with an orphan attitude approach things differently than a strong and beloved son. Many people feel like orphans in the church without sensing it. What's more, that is how many leaders feel. As I implied earlier, I think the title of pastor contributes to this problem, but it is much broader than that. So, what does an orphan heart looked like? There are great books written on this topic, but the short definition is: "the need to be validated and valued." Orphans feel a great responsibility like everything rests on their shoulders. Deep inside it's like they are the only ones they can count on, and so they have to work all the more to prove themselves and to be successful. Orphans have a hard time asking for help because it appears like weakness, but down deep inside it's because they're not sure that anyone really cares. There was a time that I wasn't aware of how much an orphan heart impacted my leadership as a pastor.

I used to have an ungodly belief that no one really cared, that the people tried to care but ultimately they just couldn't. That was an orphan heart lie. As I had been given opportunities as a spiritual leader, I had to make things happen and take advantage of every opportunity that I could create. It is not that this is entirely wrong, but it's the feeling of not been covered or protected that makes this feel so difficult. Until I was fathered, I didn't understand God's provision or generosity, but rather I had to make sure that my family's needs were being taken care of. And that's what it comes down to—it's about getting a blessing followed by the support that flows through the spirit found in true fathering and mothering. That is God's design. There is a supernatural blessing released by natural and spiritual parents that can make all the difference in our lives.

Developing relationships with spiritual mothers and fathers takes different forms and processes for different people. For some it is a very intentional process, while for others it is a matter of discovery. For Ann and me, joining Harvest International Ministry was about becoming a part of a global movement and being with those who carried the same "DNA" that we had. Being in a relationship with Ché and Sue Ahn brought a new dimension that we had not foreseen. They're true spiritual mothers and fathers in the Kingdom, and this starts with their focus on the family being a priority. I can't speak for all of the years but for the last 12 I've seen how the Ahn family lives out this priority. Their goal is to be together on Monday nights as much as possible, to vacation together every summer, to celebrate with gusto one another's birthdays, and to work side by side in the Kingdom. Ché and Sue's son and daughter-in-law, Gabriel and Monica have become the Senior Pastors of HRock Church, and their daughter Mary Ahn has become the Executive Director of HIM; the Ahn family parents are committed to raising up their own sons and daughters, as well as spiritual ones.

This sense of honor and commitment to one another is very clear to others around, and it is genuine and powerful. It has inspired me to pursue my own children as grown adults, and it has been wonderful. My daughter Loraina and her husband Glen are both part of the HIM and HRock staff family. They are being fathered and mothered in this movement. This sense of honor and commitment to one another in this family-focused movement is very clear for others to see, and it is genuine and powerful.

Early in my participation with the Ahn family, it was Gabriel Ahn, the son of Ché and Sue, that impacted me and taught me a great deal about fathering in the Kingdom. I firmly believe that this generation is called to heal their parents and grandparents. Fathering and mothering can be learned from sons and daughters, and Gabriel reached out to honor me as a spiritual father; here we are at a conference and we were asked to pair up with people of either the younger or older generation, the opposite of what each person was. It was then that Gabriel and I spoke a father-son blessing over one another. We had indeed birthed a spiritual unity.

His father, Ché, is so strong and it confused me that he would need a spiritual father. Over the years as Ché and Sue saw this relationship in action, they encouraged and celebrated it. It didn't threaten or cause weird dynamics; instead it was an extension of their own relationships and values. This taught me so much about fathering in the Kingdom. There is no jealousy or competition because the focus is on the welfare and growth of the sons and daughters. Spiritual fathers and mothers do not replace natural fathers and mothers. We are to honor the fathers and mothers of an individual regardless of how we interpret what kind of parents that they might have been. Gabriel and I, and now with his lovely wife Monica along with my wife Ann, have gone on mission trips together to eight nations in eight consecutive years. It has been Gabriel that has taught me more about honor than anyone in my life. He has been consistent, loving, encouraging, partnering, and eager to share life and ministry together. One time I asked him, "Why did you call me a spiritual father in the first place?" He simply replied that he respected me and I showed interest in him in crucial times like when he was ordained or contemplating marriage. In recent days he will explain to me, "We are in this together for life." I can't say how much and how deeply this relationship has impacted me as a spiritual father.

I came to recognize that this all started with Ché and Sue Ahn as our parents. This took time to sink in, but as always, it had been there in an underlying way. Ché never pushed the idea of him being my father onto me. He spoke honestly to me about my orphan heart, and at times was very firm in telling me that I was acting in an unhealthy way. For example, there was a time when HIM was struggling financially and Ché did everything he could not to let anyone go. As a leader, he wanted to set an example and took a financial cut himself. He asked me to do the same. My initial response was about the money and how could I make ends meet. Ché said to me as a father, "Why did you go to the money first? It tells me that you do not understand your Heavenly Father as your provider." He was right. I didn't understand Kingdom finance because of the problems and wounds in my own heart.

Another time, Ché spoke to me about giving. He said to me directly, "Apostles start their giving at 20% and go up from there," a belief that Ché and Sue live out by giving

51%+ of their income to the Lord and Kingdom purposes every year, with the goal of giving 90%. This kind of parenting has changed my entire life and relationship with finances. It has increased my trust in the Lord, my faith in his provision, and to be more generous and joyous in giving. Ché and Sue have been an example of the following principles: to prioritize family, to focus on the Kingdom, and to release others in ministry with honor and giving. They are amazing examples and I appreciate them as spiritual parents.

In sharing this testimony I must say it wasn't always easy. I failed to see the orphan thinking that had been hindering my ministry and relationships. Looking back, we had been working together for about ten years. For most of those years, I perceived them more as older siblings, my covering, my spiritual leaders, and as friends. They were all of those things. At first it felt awkward to call them parents, maybe because in my mind I wanted to preserve the friendship and not put on false expectations. Here is the important part...they had no expectations for that. They simply were faithful and true to themselves. They didn't need me to call them parents, because for them it's like everything else in their lives, meaning that it isn't about what we say or about titles. I can now say with great joy and relief that Ché and Sue Ahn are our spiritual parents as well as amazing friends.

It takes an open and willing heart to be "fathered," and it isn't always easy. The spiritual parents we have won't be perfect, and depending on their style it won't always feel warm and fuzzy. The goal is to position your heart for God to use spiritual leaders to point us to Himself. This is another example and key aspect for relational transformation to take place in your life.

A New Title that Changed Me: "Papa Mark"

Around 2012 something started to shift in our movement. About that time some people started calling me "Papa Mark"... it surprised me. Up until that time it was sometimes awkward for people to know exactly how to address me. Should they call me apostle, or pastor, or maybe prophet? I generally told people they can call me whatever they want to, and often joked "just call me dude." But when they started calling me Papa Mark, a part of me did not know how to receive it. While I feel like overall I had been a good father to my children, I have struggled at times keeping my heart open when they were disobedient or rebellious. This has caused some regret in me, because the bottom line is I want to love and have a great relationship with my own children. God really wanted me to receive this role in people's lives and to affirm the title of Papa Mark. I prayed about it and asked the Lord to teach me. I never expected the following to happen, but it did. For 21 days straight someone either called me on the phone, told me in person, or wrote in an e-mail that I was their spiritual father. I literally had people get on their knees crying and telling me I was their father. It was humbling and amazingly wonderful.

It was not a coincidence that the same thing was happening with Ché Ahn. Suddenly, everyone was calling him Papa as well. I am convinced it was a God thing, because He was teaching us about the apostolic movement. As leaders, The Lord wants us to have His heart for His people. When we look at titles like apostle or prophet from the traditional church's perspective, they have nuances that can cause apprehension. But the title Papa carries less baggage and has a common translation worldwide. I love it when people tell me that I have the heart of a Papa.

Recently, I was in Northern India with some amazing leaders that have planted over 2000 house churches. They don't have titles nor do they receive special recognition. They just go out daily after their teaching job is over, with the goal of winning one or two more villages for Christ. One day as I prayed for this wonderful couple, I simply told them how proud of them that I was. This precious Indian woman laid her head on my shoulder and said, "I never have had a Papa. Thank you so much for your love." I want to say humbly that over the last decade, and especially the last five years I have heard that sentiment over and over again. What it tells me is they see the love of the heavenly Father in me. What a great honor and privilege that is. It means the world to me. If this is what it means to be an apostle, I want it. Remember it is all about function. When I am called "Papa," it even feels greater than the title apostle. I firmly believe that my greatest titles are first, "Son"; second, "Brother"; third, "Papa." ... "Husband" is in their somewhere, too, as it is the love of my wife, her faith and strength that have changed me. My wife Ann is an amazing wife and mother. She has a deep love for her natural and spiritual children that inspires and teaches me.

Complications With the Title Father

I also like to joke that it is only in Spanish that this title is a problem, because papas in Spanish means potatoes. Have people been calling us potatoes? Seriously though, this process hasn't happened without complications. Folks can be quick to call me father but I've learned that it isn't always healthy. What kind of expectations do they have, and what are they really saying? Conversely, you can lead others who never called me papa or father, but they positioned themselves as son and daughters. What I mean by this is that they relate to you in such an expression of honor that they believed that God is going to give them an impartation of His heart through you. As with the Gabriel

Ahn example earlier, it is really about what is called sonship, the relation between a father and his son. In other words, to become a great father we need to know how to be a son. Even though Jesus was one with the Father, He clearly did not position Himself as an equal (Philippians 2), but as One who was submitted yielded to the Father. Jesus meant it when He said the Son can do nothing by Himself. Think about the honor and commitment that this was by Jesus.

Again, reflect on the significance of this declaration by Jesus. This shows us the role of sonship here on earth. When we talk about apostolic fathering, this must be a reality in the apostle's life. The reason is it sets the tone. It is about humility and looking to the Heavenly Father in everything. As the Lord increases our authority and establishes us as Spiritual fathers and mothers, we are to point everyone to the Heavenly Father. Jesus is our example, and he taught us how to be sons and daughters. When we talk about apostolic fathering, this must be a reality in the apostles life. As spiritual fathers and mothers, we must always direct people to rely on the Lord. Spiritual parents never replace the natural parents. We always direct others to the Father and reflect His love the best we can.

Here is an additional concern about this teaching. We can't create a false expectation that we are going to be there for everyone that sees us as their spiritual fathers or mothers. That is unrealistic and creates another opportunity for people to be hurt. When someone calls me a father, it means that they honor me and want to receive from me the Father's love and His blessing. It doesn't mean I will now step in and be everything they hoped a father would be that their natural father was not. I know that seems obvious, but there are lot of people who are desperately needing approval of a father and mother they never received. It still shocks me how quickly people reach out to me as a father, and I and blessed by that, but it shows me the huge vacuum and needs that are in people's heart. When people call me father, I try to share what that means and does not mean to me. I don't want to set people up to look to me in a way that is unhealthy for them, and to put undue pressure on our relationship that God never intended. Leaders that need this love and approval from the people become vulnerable to committing spiritual abuse, in some cases sexual impropriety. That is how primal and basic the need for fathers and mothers is. This is all the more reason why we should understand the importance of becoming spiritual fathers and mothers as well as the equipping others to do the same.

My Spiritual Son, Simon

With this background I want to tell you some amazing stories that show us these principles as well as the power of spiritual fathering and mothering. One of the major joys in parenting has been with our spiritual son Simon from Kenya. Since the year 2000, he has been the primary contact and coordinator for us in Africa. He is an example of someone who really positioned himself as a son. The title of Papa is actually used for foreigners, as well as the title Mama. This is a way of simply showing respect to an older person who shows care toward you. When it comes to the church and mission's use of titles, they have actually been used to manipulate foreigners. It brings a quicker trust and sense of family to their relationship, but often the case is not real. There are some who are sincere, but it is common for pastors to call someone papa and speak glowing words of their loyalty and dedication while they are present. Yet when the guest leaves and another one comes they may receive the same accolades and statements of affection as the former. Simon was different from the very beginning. Unlike many other situations, he made it clear that he was not seeking money as his main goal. I don't say this lightly, but in the case of Kenya, everyone prays for someone to come and sponsored them and take care of their needs, ranging from the ministry to personal needs. They are very desperate.

Simon was a school teacher with a consistent income. The late Bishop Joseph is someone who was in the ministry but also conducted outside businesses and was not fully dependent on the church. These examples are rare in Kenya, where business men and women are actually viewed as less spiritual because they are not building up first and foremost a church. There is a dichotomy in the minds of many Kenyan leaders, which creates a tension between business and ministry. The result is that pastors are often viewed as beggars, and it's a commonly accepted practice for the leaders to quote the foreign guests inflated costs in conducting ministry and conferences. This practice is how they help support themselves and why you may even receive an e-mail requesting that you to come into meetings in the country with people you never met or even heard of. The goal is to bring money to their ministry but it is partly the fault of western leaders who buy into this deception. I'm not against helping in supporting leaders financially, but this must be done with great wisdom and caution. How can giving money to a worthy cause be harmful? The short answer is that this is generally the cause for competition, deception, and an unhealthy dependence. To be effective spiritual fathers and mothers, we must teach leaders in other nations that we are not there to simply finance their dreams, but rather to equip them and help them build and raise up a ministry that is dependent on the Lord.

This is why my relationship with Simon has been so healing to me. When we would come to his country, he would take time off from his school work and, along with us, would devote himself to building the Kingdom and the network of Rock Creek Church. When Bishop Joseph passed away, the denomination asked me to come to Kenya to assist in commissioning a successor. I had been openly recommending Simon to be that person, and before his passing, Bishop Joseph confirmed this. Simon did call me "Papa" and Ann "Mama" from the beginning. But it wasn't simply something he said with his mouth. It was how he lived it out. He communicated with us frequently, was highly accountable when he was given money to steward, and he demonstrated a heart for not only his own denomination but for the entire body of Christ. After we would do a conference and would return home, he would take the topic and make it his own and then go into remote villages to share the messages that we had brought. Every time we returned to visit for conferences, there were always many leaders and churches eager to receive us and for the right reasons.

Here is the power of this: our relationship as spiritual fathers and mothers was impacting the movement we began together. After commissioning Simon as the Bishop of a denomination, I also appointed him in a new role that was in conjunction with mine. I had gone from the local church ministry as a Senior Pastor to the Executive Director of Harvest International Ministry. With the agreement of those from Rock Creek Church we changed the name of the Rock Creek Churches to Kenya, Harvest International Ministry. The reason was because I was the spiritual father, an apostle to the movement in Kenya. A key aspect of this was that Simon was my spiritual son, and we have worked closely together for many years and seen the churches grow in virtually every region of Kenya.

Regarding finances, it was not until 2014 that Simon left his job as a school teacher in faith and began to receive finances from myself and other HIM sources. For his 14 years of service before that point, we can clearly say that it was not about money at all. The only reason this change was made was so Simon was freed to do the full-time work of an apostle. It wasn't a coincidence that Papa Ché Ahn visited Kenya for the first time. His main purpose was to commission Simon as an Apostle with me. We gave the ministry away totally. When he calls me on the phone, or we prepare for a trip, I say to him, "Simon, how can I serve you when I come?" I realized that it must be Kenyans leading Kenyans. Guess what happened after we commissioned him as the Apostle? We went from 1,000 churches in Kenya to over 3,000 in 2.5 years!

He and his wife Selena have been an amazing joy in this whole season. Others who called us father and mother constantly asked us for money and distanced themselves if they did not receive what they wanted. I actually understand they need support, but I felt convicted that the old wine skin actually hurts the people. It creates and sustains a poverty mindset that teaches the people they are poor and unable to do what they need to do. We taught Simon about business and he now has several businesses with his wife, one of which is raising cattle. A couple of years ago he said to Ann and I with excitement, "I have something I want to show you." He drove out into the outskirts of Kilifi to a field where the cattle were roaming. He went to one and pointed out it saying, "Papa and Mama, this is your cow." In Kenyan spiritual culture, first-fruit-offerings are given to spiritual fathers and mothers. Simon honored us with his finances and to this day we have a growing herd of cattle in Kenya.

During our last visit to Kenya we went to his home and spent time with his wife and children. They called me "Babu," which is grandfather, and Ann "Nyanya," which is grandmother. It gave me a picture of our role in Kenya and I shared this in subsequent meetings. To illustrate this new role to the Kenyans, I put Simon on top of my shoulders while preaching. It showed that my heart is to lift of my son and to serve them as a "Babu." It was very effective and meaningful for the people. Thank you, Lord, for strategies and ideas!

More than One Father

You may recall how Papa Ché graciously responded to my relationship with Gabriel. That was an important principal that is special in our movement. God will, in His time, bring other leaders into our spiritual son's and daughter's lives, and they too will be considered their spiritual fathers and mothers. Some want to limit this to one father, usually the one who led the person to Christ. However, our faith journey is made up of different stages of development, and God will use different leaders at different times to take us into the new things that we need to learn and grow in. The Apostle Paul wrote in first Corinthians 4:15 that they have many teachers but few fathers. I think it is important to note that the word "fathers" is plural. So, in Kenya there have been other apostles that have joined me and carried the vision that we have to that nation. One is named Bruce Lindley from the Gold Coast of Australia. He is primarily a long-term son of Ché Ahn, but he has acknowledged me as one of his fathers as well. The main way he showed this was by partnering with me and traveling to numerous nations, carrying my heart. He brought things to the movement in Kenya that I could not bring. But this is how the Kingdom works; God uses different leaders, including a plural number of apostles and fathers in different ways and seasons. Simon calls Bruce, "Papa," and acknowledges him as an apostle, and I celebrate this relationship and all that has brought to the people of Kenya. Bruce and Cheryl were commissioned as HIM apostles several years ago and continue to support our work in Kenya, especially with the orphanage located in Kilifi, Kenya.

I have heard inquiries such as, "Doesn't that cause problems when you have more than one father?" The truth is, it can cause problems if the fathers and mothers don't honor one another, or if they are working against each other, or if one feels the need to be more important than another one. If, however, there is no competition and honor is highly valued, it actually works quite well. We have a large number of leaders in our ministry that acknowledge not only Ché and myself as fathers, but also other significant apostles in our movement as well. Consider how a father like myself views the whole picture. I make it clear to everyone that Ché is my apostle and father. Or put differently, he is my primary apostle and spiritual father. I don't need to call someone my secondary one, but in my heart I know where I am accountable and whom God has aligned my life with. I will speak more about alignment in another chapter because it is essential truth to a movement. However, the question is, "Whom has God picked for you to align with?"

In the case of Simon, there has never been confusion as to who his primary spiritual parents are (Ann and me). At the same time, we give high honor to Bruce Lindley, as he too is one of Simon's spiritual fathers. Simon and the movement are blessed because of this. That is why it is easy to celebrate.

I keep on using this word honor, which we know means respect and high regard. But let's also look at how we use the word when we say that someone honors a contract. Simply, they act in accordance with the agreed to commitments of that contract. When a person honors a leader, their goal is to be in accordance with the spirit in their heart regarding matters which are shared. And that goes in both the horizontal and vertical directions. For example, when Gabriel Ahn and I travel together, we have the goal of out-honoring each another. It appears that we might be joking, but we really mean it. We say, "I know I honor you." Then the other one will say, "I honor you." This is lived out on trips, too. Sometimes we will look at a situation and say, "This is about your growth and I want to defer to you." This happened in Brazil when I saw a new mantle falling on Gabriel and Monica for that nation (Monica is from Brazil). However, when we were in Bulgaria, Gabriel felt he should defer to me because he saw the father anointing being released in a great way through me. Bruce and I honor Papa Ché, and so that is the foundation of our ability to honor one another. This is one of the core reasons I believe that being a part of a global movement is far better than ministering on your own and building your own section of the Kingdom somewhere.

A Radical Pastor Named Frederick

Around 2011, there was a young man from Uganda named Frederick. This story illustrates many principles of what it means to be a son first and then a father in the Kingdom. He was raised in the Palissa District of northeastern Uganda. He was not unlike most other young men or women who have the goal of going to the city and getting a college degree and building a better life with the conveniences of having running water and electricity. Through faith and family support he was able to go to Kampala and get a college education. Frederick wanted to serve God, and he fought the tension between business and ministry that I shared earlier. So, in addition to having a job, he started a church in his home where he was building the kind of life that most would only dream of. But there came a time when he thought that God told him he was to return back to the rural areas and help the people in the land where he grew up. When he arrived back in the area, people asked him why he returned. Many thought he was foolish to return back to where he came from.

Frederick started a church and it began to grow as he shared with the people much of what he had learned. During this time they aspired to have what every church and Uganda wants to have...a roof. That's right, before you get walls you need to have a roof. A basic roof is made by binding corrugated galvanized sheets and to attach them to the tops of large poles that are put into the ground. Fred knew that to accomplish this goal, the church had to put it as a priority and provide finances. His idea was for everyone in the church to fast one day a week and bring the money saved for an offering that would be dedicated to the roof. After one year, the church received enough money to make a large roof which was suitable to provide covering from the sun and rain. After they purchased the corrugated sheets, Fred planned for a dedication service for the sheets. The stock size for the sheets is four by eight feet, the same as plywood. They purchased 80 of the tin sheets and prepared for a dedication service.

As Fred prayed, he heard the Lord tell him to give away all eighty sheets. He went back to the Lord thinking he had not heard correctly and said, "You mean eight of them as a tithe, right?" But the Lord reported back quickly, "No, you heard me right, give me all eighty of them." So Frederick obeyed and went to many of the neighboring churches in the region and gave away all eighty sheets, giving two to five each to varying churches all over the county. When the people of his church saw this, they were infuriated, as they had invested their lives for one year into the project. They yelled at him, "We thought you were crazy when you left the city, but now we know you are." Everyone in his church abandoned him and left for other places.

Perhaps Frederick could have handled this differently, but he wanted to be obedient and felt that it was God who had led him. After his people rejected him, Frederick was in total despair and discouragement. He had left the city only to be a failure. In a state of desperation, Frederick rented a small room and before entering it, he told his wife that he was going to go into the room for 21 days to get an answer from God. As he went into the room, he locked it and slid the key back under the door. He told his wife to come back for him in 21 days and he would have the revelation of what to do. I can't imagine what Frederick did to survive in that room all that time, but when he tells the story he said the Spirit led him to pray a prayer:

Paraphrasing, here was his cry: "Father, I no longer want to be an orphan!" In Romans 8, the Apostle Paul tells us that when we do not know how to pray, the Holy Spirit intercedes and groans for us. This prayer captured the essence of what Frederick needed to pray. A change was needed...the Lord had a new wineskin for him. For me, even though I did not to use the phrase in that exact way, it was the key for my life and possibly for yours. We can no longer be orphans in our heart or spirit. For Frederick, it was this prayer that broke in and revealed his true condition. As long as a leader acts like an orphan and does not really known true sonship with God, it will hinder his life and ministry in ways he won't understand.

What happened next staggers the mind. Frederick had a vision. This is a strange one, but Frederick saw the Harvest International Ministry web site, specifically, "www.harvestim.org." It sounds crazy, but it affirms that God can use the Internet...amen! There's more. He also had a vision of a white man that was heavy-set and had a beard, which is a pretty good description of yours truly. He saw me and the Lord told him that through me, many fathers would come to him and help him establish what God had planned for him. To be literal, he said when recounting his vision, "The first man [who he thinks is Jesus] entered the room and it seemed like he was literally in the room. Following, I appeared in the room as well!" To verify the details of this story, I met with him in May of 2017 to confirm each aspect of the vision.

It is important to say that Frederick had never heard of me or Harvest International Ministry before this time.

When he finally went to the website, he was in awe that it even existed. So he opened the homepage and asked through the contact form for direction on what to do. The office pointed him to Simon Karisa in Kenya, who not only oversaw that nation, but is our HIM Africa Director. When Simon received an e-mail from Frederick, he invited him to come and meet with him and promised to give him materials that would be a strength to him. This, of course, was the Bible school material that we had commissioned Simon to give away to everyone he could. Neither Simon nor Frederick understood the significance of the meeting at the time, but Frederick took both the meeting and the material as a confirmation from God that he had heard correctly during his 21 days of solitary confinement in the locked room. Upon returning home, which involved a 30 to 40 hour bus ride, Frederick begin to devour the materials. He remembered that Simon had told him, "If you want to grow in the Kingdom and in your leadership, give this material away to others as you are able." He did exactly that—he began by going to the churches that he had given that corrugated sheets to. Their hearts were open and they trusted Frederick. He had done something that they had never seen before when he gave the sheets away to so many people. Numerous churches received him, and in the process they fed and housed him and cared for him in love.

What was happening? Frederick was now moving in an apostolic ministry without realizing it. It wasn't until later when he finished studying the material and the fivefold ministry that it dawned on him that he was on an apostolic ministry journey. There was so much favor coming his way that he asked Simon to come and see what he was doing, and if he could start a Harvest International Ministry Office for his region. Frederick was serving everyone he could in the region. The local churches believed that he had their best interests in mind, so they began to honor him as a spiritual leader and father. Prior to actually starting a church, he was about conducting meetings and holding conferences that were open to all leaders. He taught people to honor their spiritual leaders and fathers, for the problem was that many of the leaders were begging for money and controlling their people. When Fred began his ministry, he knew that he had to have new wine skins for the new wine teaching of empowering and equipping the people. The time came for a Harvest International Ministry conference in Kenya. Simon invited him to come as a special guest from Uganda. When Frederick was at a conference meeting, he looked on the stage and there was the man he had seen in his vision (yours truly). He was overwhelmed. He was so excited that he could come and meet me and tell me his story, as well as to invite me to see and bless his ministry.

Another shocker...the Holy Spirit came upon him and he fell to the ground and he couldn't speak for three days. The conference ended, we left, and he returned home unable to share with me or anyone else that I was the one in the vision. When he prayed, he cried out to the Lord, "Why did you do that?" The Father said to him, "To become a father in the Kingdom, you must learn to be a son first. If you look to one earthly man to meet all of your needs, you won't understand what fathering in the Kingdom is. I will use this man, and then others, but you will not meet him until you are ready, otherwise you would just look to him in an improper way." That really says all. It is all about the proper placing of faith and trust in our Heavenly Father. Then the Lord promised Frederick, "When you're ready, I will send this man to you without you even asking him."

I am blown away by Frederick's amazing relationship with God. After some time Simon went and saw what Frederick was doing, and was very encouraged by it. In this time frame, Frederick had gathered many churches and unified them in the region, plus his own ministries had grown significantly.

Every time I travel to Africa I asked my spiritual son Simon to tell me where I should go and what I should do. Even though he is my son, he's the one that carries and oversees the ministry. So on this occasion Simon told me, there is a man named Frederick who has the ministry in Uganda, and I think he is ready for a visit from you. Frederick had not told Simon the story, because he trusted the Father to do as He said He would. That year, around 2012, I took along with me a powerful HIM pastor from the Vancouver, B.C. area, whose name is Steven Kim.

This was in part due to what happened in Uganda. Going there was a part of his training to become an apostle. He is a very good teacher on the topic of fathering, and he brought a strong and zealous team with him from his church.

It was incredible when Steve got up to teach because it was similar to my experience when I first went to Kenya. I could literally see the mantle of the apostolic falling on Steve going into a whole new level, and I wasn't the only one that saw this. Everyone from his church was marveling of what they were witnessing. Pastor Steve had done everything he could to align himself with a Papa Ché and as a part of that honored me is one of his fathers. It was a reminder and encouragement of my calling and destiny to raise up other leaders, especially those in the apostolic. Steve and Sonya were later commissioned by Harvest International Ministry as an apostle, and he has continued to go to Uganda since developing his own network of churches and relationships. He now has a ministry not only to church leaders, but also to business and government leaders there.

Commanding Blessings and the Rain Came!

After he spoke, I got up and the Spirit came with a mighty force. He told me to speak to all the heavenlies in every direction of the compass, and to command that every spiritual blessing that had been withheld by the enemy to be released into the atmosphere. This wasn't normal language for me to hear, but it was very specific as I heard it. I took my arm and pointed to the north and said, "I come and every spiritual blessing that has been withheld from these people to be released in Jesus' name." Then I spoke in the same way facing the east, then south, and then west, each time declaring an apostolic decree according to the Word of the Lord.

I truly did not know what it really meant. However, I got to see a glimpse in just about 15 minutes. There had been a severe drought in the area for over six months in which they had seen no rain. Shortly after I made this declaration, you could feel a sudden wind flowing in small circles, and within minutes the blue skies began to gather rain clouds right above our heads. Frankly, I wasn't focusing on commanding rain, but as I released the blessings I knew the rain was a part of it.

The people knew exactly what was happening and they began to respond in faith. They brought forward a young woman in her twenties that was a quadriplegic. She had never walked or sat up and could not move her arms or legs. The rain began as a drizzle and slowly increased. It was a gift from God. Meanwhile, we remained in a mode of prayer and thanksgiving. As prayer for this woman intensified, the power of God began to enter her body. She then began to move to the amazement of those around. Before long, she sat up and then stood up for the first time in her life. Many people came forth by faith to receive their healing.

One memorable one was a young girl around 12 years old that had been born totally deaf and her speech was unintelligible. After we prayed, her ears were opened. She then began to speak with clarity and could be heard by everyone around us. I'll never forget their reaction. They didn't comment at first on the fact that she could hear, but that when she spoke she was intelligent. They were amazed and said they thought she was mentally retarded because when she tried to speak, it sounded like a baby battling. Imagine this...you are a 12 year deaf old girl; you wake up on any normal day, and suddenly you can hear and speak clearly with intelligence.

Many more exciting things happened that day, but I want to get to the heart of the story. This story is about sonship, about looking to your Heavenly Father and entrusting your life and every area of your ministry with Him. We were all benefiting from the faith and obedience of Frederick. Miracles were occurring. Here is another example. While in the region, I had a hired man who was our "designated driver." It is common in East Africa to have such a driver because he knew the way around the terrain and it was also safer. One day I turned to my driver, Kephous, a kind and gentle fellow, and older than Frederick. I sensed that he was a man of integrity and influence, and I asked him, "What do you do for a living? You're a good driver but I sense that there is a lot more to you." He said, "I am an overseer in a denomination with over 10,000 churches in Uganda." I marveled at this and replied, "And you are my driver?" He responded, "I wanted to meet and see the man that would come out with a team from America into the rural areas of Africa to help my brother Frederick. I have been listening to your teaching the last few days, and our team of overseers has been praying for revelation on how to organize our fast-growing movement. I believe you are an answer to our prayers. Will you please return and we will gather leaders from our entire nation for this training on the fivefold ministry?"

Wow, isn't that like God? We did return the next year and began training with Kephous and the leaders of that movement. Frederick has grown in stature and he is leading a great movement in Eastern Uganda, and has been a part of the Harvest International Ministry team in Africa. Kephous is now leading the Global Joy network in Uganda under the leadership of Apostle Steve Kim and New Joy Church.

It is stunning to think that all of this was a result of one man willing to give away his roof sheets. At the end of our time with him, Frederick shared the story of how he had his vision in that room. He waited to the end because he didn't want to manipulate me in any way, and that he trusted the Lord to be his provider first and foremost. Frederick has grown in stature and he is leading a great movement in Eastern Uganda, and he has been a part of the Harvest International Ministry team in East Africa. Other fathers and leaders have gone to him and he is highly respected in the region. He now has over 250 churches in the HIM network.

In the last five years, God has been teaching me the importance of fully understanding my role as a spiritual father and my wife's role as a spiritual mother. The enemy tried to defeat me from this as he knew my weaknesses and limitations as a natural father. No father is perfect, but I am inspired to improve as a natural father. Since I became more aware of this role in the Kingdom, it motivated me to pursue my natural children in a greater way. During this season, I have grown closer to each one of them as they grow into adulthood. I do pray that they will come into the fullness that God has prepared for them.

It is true that we will make mistakes as spiritual fathers and mothers, just like we do in the natural. I have made some mistakes along the way, and encourage anyone who wants to be a spiritual father and mother to be accountable to their spouses and to keep appropriate boundaries with our spiritual kids.

A pitfall can occur when people call you a father without it having merit. They may be looking for someone to love and accept them, but they may be asking for more than you are able to give. Help others, but be honest about what this concept means, and how it only grows over time through honor, loyalty, and respect. When it comes to ministering to young women, my wife Ann becomes very involved. Ann has spiritual sons that need love not only from a father but from a mother as well. We therefore ask that all correspondence such as emails be directed to both of us. We talk about this as needed, and we minister jointly in most cases where the opposite gender is involved. We don't want to nurture an unhealthy dependence on us and, as always, have been blessed as God has filled me with His love for sons and daughters.

Do You Really Want Me to Be Your Spiritual Father?

I have another son I want to tell you about, because it shows the influence that the father can have and the impact it can have on many. I worked rather casually with one of our churches in Southern California for about a year, until one day I had lunch with the senior pastor. It was actually a difficult season for him and as we talked he poured out his heart and became vulnerable. He told me that he respected me and looked to me in part as a spiritual father, which I really hadn't realized to that point. During this season I spoke at his church and led a men's retreat. This is another example on how a person can align as a son and it leads to a great relationship where God can use it to bring healing. At the men's retreat, I got to know some of the other pastors on his team, and one of them was seeking God for a spiritual father. After I spoke that weekend, I sensed that he was intensely inquiring of the Lord about this, and he mentioned it to me. I told him that I would be honored, and since his senior pastor was aligned, it was very fitting. We kept in some contact but it was very informal and sporadic. He didn't have too high of an expectation.

A number of months later, this same associate pastor picked me up at the airport. On the way to the church, he was telling me about the growing conflict over the senior pastor in his church. Many other people in his small group plus a few others were complaining to him. People were telling him that he should be the senior pastor and that the current one should resign because of the things he was doing. There was no accusation of sin, merely minor issues that were causing the controversy. I knew in my heart that the associate was in a spiritual battle, and that he, unknowingly, was part of the problem. I firmly believe that what we sow is what we reap.

I then asked him a question, and with feeling. "Did you mean it when you said that you want me to be your spiritual father? Because right now if you mean that, it's going to release me to give you a genuine answer for your problem." With his permission, in love, I went after him. I told him that he had a covenant with the senior pastor, and reminded him that they had been partners for nearly 12 years. They started the church together, and he was his partner. Without knowing it, he had become wounded and divided from the senior pastor. Church people were using him to vent their problems with the ultimate goal that he would be their solution to help them get rid of the senior pastor. I told him in no uncertain terms that he had to repent and to go to the senior pastor and become reunited and renew their covenant. I also spoke to the senior pastor and told him that he had hurt the associate and that he too needed to take on the spirit of humility. I'm happy to say that both of them did repent and renewed their love and covenant.

This is the role of the spiritual father; he can say in love what the sons need to hear, but ultimately it is the role of the sons and daughters to receive and apply what they hear.

Getting back to the story. In the end, the group that was in opposition sought out another associate to use as their instrument and he had his own grievances and problems. But the senior and the associate stayed together and learned so much about the power of unity and of submitting themselves to another person in their ministry. The church did go through a hard time, but the leadership stayed unified overall, and they grew in maturity in their apostolic role. It is such an honor and joy to be one of their spiritual fathers.

In the Spring of 2017, the senior pastor of this church was led by the Spirit to resign. The associate was ready to lead, but he knew it had to be by the Spirit and not by his hand. He patiently waited as the church prayed and worked through the process. The leaders commented on his humility and ability to lead by example. The church extended the offer to become the senior pastor. Pastor Joe called me and said, "Papa, I want you to come and lay hands on me and install me." I felt so honored and had the blessing of praying for Joe and Andrea in their installation service, in June 2017.

I wanted to share this story because I learned a lot about the role of fathering through them. Because I trust Pastor Joe, I recently went to the associate for inner healing prayer. The former senior leader continues to teach me about honoring and generosity. He too means a lot me.

Fathering in Europe

In the Spring of 2014, we were visiting an apostolic center aligned with HIM in Amsterdam, The Netherlands. The founding apostles there are Dick and Arleen Westerhof. They lead God's Embassy Church. They organized an event entitled "Activating the Apostolic," and invited leaders from churches in the region. It was my first time ministering in The Netherlands. When we drove up to the church I suddenly felt the Father's love for them and began to weep. The Lord said, "They have many teachers, but few fathers." The Lord told me clearly that merging of the apostolic and fathering could transform the nation. As I began the day, I told them that the Lord wanted me to minister to their hearts as a "father." I wasn't claiming to be their father, but instead I was representing the Heavenly Father. The Spirit fell and many were touched and testified later that healing took place.

Another memorable story took place in Bulgaria in the fall of 2015. There we were, with an apostolic leader, Ivodor. This man is a mighty apostle who is transforming the prison system. As we worked with him and poured out love as apostolic fathers, he became overwhelmed. He said, "Is this real or is it an illusion? Because we came out of Communism, my generation are the forerunners; we have no fathers. I opened my heart to an American man 25 years ago to be a father, but he used my ministry to raise money and didn't even give it to me. But you and your team are pouring so much love into us and wanting nothing in return. You and your spiritual son Gabriel have such a special relationship and you are sharing it with me and my people. We are being changed."

This is God's design. It begins with the natural family and goes to the church family. When Paul said there weren't many fathers in I Corinthians 4:15, this is what he said: "Even if you had ten thousand guardians in Christ, you do not have many fathers, for in Christ Jesus I became your father through the gospel." What a bold statement, "I became your father through the gospel." It tells us that Paul had this understanding and he took the role seriously, "I am your father." In Philippians 2:19-22, Paul wrote, "I hope in the Lord Jesus to send Timothy to you soon, that I also may be cheered when I receive news about you. I have no one else like him, who will show genuine concern for your welfare. For everyone looks out for their own interests, not those of Jesus Christ. But you know that Timothy has proved himself, because as a son with his father he has served with me in the work of the gospel." Paul asserts that this is a special relationship, a proven one where we work together closely and with deep trust.

Fathers and Sons in the Kingdom

The greatest power of these verses is where Paul relates the relationship of a son and father in the Kingdom. It is the picture of family that ministered to Paul's heart and enabled him to chase and pursue his purpose. Paul used this language of family often. It wasn't just partners, it was family. For example in Galatians 6:1, "Therefore, as we have opportunity, let us do good to all people, especially to those who belong to the family of believers." Many people have never experienced the joy of a close and healthy family. God invites us to be a family, well more specifically, His family. Paul wrote in Ephesians 3, "For this reason I kneel before the Father, from whom every family in heaven and on earth derives its name." The Greek word for family, *patria*, is derived from the Greek word for father, *pater*. So God's word connects the concept of God as our Heavenly Father. He is the One who Fathers us and leads us. God is the one that from the beginning established the family with a father. In Genesis 2:24, "That is why a man leaves his father and mother and is united to his wife, and they become one flesh." Do you know what is strange about this verse? Adam and Eve did not have a father and mother! So, why is it there? Because he was establishing the divine order for the family even before it happened. God appointed the father and mother to raise their children into maturity, and at such a time, they would leave them and establish their own families. The goal is to raise up mature sons and daughters who will then do the same.

Here is the problem we face. Many people are not mature as fathers and mothers, because they themselves were never fathered or mothered. That is the damage that sin did. Sin came against this cycle, and as a result fathers and mothers have passed their sins down through the generations. Everywhere I go, I find very capable leaders who are anointed and have zeal, and who want to make a difference. However, the abandonment and lack of emotion and relationship has created wounds that are profoundly deep. When it comes to the apostolic, this has been very detrimental, because many apostles have been controlling, abusive, and self-promoting. They had the title but did not function as fathers.

But let me share this: the fathers get wounded too. They are wounded. They don't give the love and covering because they never got it. Quite frankly, they don't know how. They don't realize the power of our words and actions. That is why apostolic fathering is key in transforming the church and the world. We are called to be different, we are called to lead the way. For this to happen we need to be healed, grow in maturity, and learn to relate differently. In other words, we need to develop the heart and the skills to do so. We need to learn what it means to be spiritual fathers and mothers. We can't ignore or downplay the importance of this. What about your life and ministry? Who are your spiritual fathers and mothers, and are you demonstrating honor to them? Who are you called to be a spiritual parent to and have you intentionally defined what that looks like? Spiritual parenting is vital in the process of relational transformation.

Healing of my Heart

I want to share this occurrence in my life. In 2010, I went to a church named "New Joy" in Richmond, B.C., and did a class on the fivefold ministry. I stayed over for the Sunday service and preached on Father's Day, and to my surprise I was treated with the honor of a father. I was given Father's Day gifts and love was poured onto me. I asked why they were doing this? Pastor Steven and Sonya Kim said that as a part of HIM, they took the role of fathers very seriously. Ché Ahn is their primary father, but they extended this honor toward me. I did not realize then, but God was beginning a year of impartation regarding apostolic fathering. God was initiating sons and daughters that were going to be used by God to bring a healing into my own life. Less than a month later, I hired two women to work in my office. I did not know at the time, but both had fathers that were in the ministry but had affairs and had left them at an early age. Soon after working for me, they started to call me "Papa Mark." One of the woman in particular began to access a part of my heart that had only previously belonged to one person, my natural daughter Loraina. This was my first glimpse of the power of relationship with a spiritual daughter.

A few months later, the Holy Spirit began to escalate this. I preached a sermon at HRock on overcoming worldly sorry and regret. I asked the Holy Spirit to reveal what I regretted the most and what He wanted to heal. He said, "Your relationship with your son." He told me something that I already knew, but had avoided the truth. One of my children pushed all the wrong buttons, and I battled with keeping my heart open to him. If you look at Malachi 4:6, it tells us what happens if the father's heart is turned away or closed from the sons, and if the son's hearts are closed to the fathers: there is a curse. This condition has caused immense pain in my family. Even though we loved Jesus, and were in many ways a loving family, there was a wound centered around the inability for this relationship to be fully led by the Spirit.

This is an important truth. Out of pain, we can actually close our hearts to our sons and daughters. Consider the following verses from 2 Corinthians 6: "We have spoken freely to you, Corinthians, and opened wide our hearts to you. We are not withholding our affection from you, but you are withholding yours from us. As a fair exchange—I speak as to my children—open wide your hearts also."

So, the Lord spoke to me on January 2nd (I remember the day). "Son, this year you are going to see your relationship healed with your son!" A few minutes later, I asked the Lord about the theme of the year. It is a practice that I do. He said, "You are going to learn how to give and receive unconditional love in a way you have never experienced."

The next day the attack came against this word. Ann and I confronted this son about some things he was doing in our home. He lost his temper and went way over the line. We contemplated harsh consequences, but after a few moments, the Holy Spirit said, "What did I say yesterday? You will give and receive unconditional love in a way you have never before." While I was praying, the Holy Spirit said to me, "Give him no consequence and ask him to forgive you for not showing the unconditional love of the Father." So I called him upstairs, along with Ann and his twin brother, and I told both my boys that it was my desire to show them the Father's love in a new way. It impacted all of us and there were tears shed. In essence, the Lord turned my heart to my children.

If you want to be an apostolic father, it begins with your heart toward your own children. I have made it my goal for the last five years to pursue all of them more than I ever have before. They have noticed it and commented positively about it. Our relationship isn't perfect, but we have all grown in the process and I believe our relationships will continue to grow and improve.

The next step continued when I went back up to New Joy during the first week of March in 2011. This time I taught a breakthrough class for Wagner University (Wagner Leadership Institute at the time), and during that class I cried out for this area in my own life too. I wanted a breakthrough as a father. During the fellowship time Pastor Sonya had shared with me about Restoring the Foundation ministry that she led in the church. In my heart, I wanted to go to her for inner healing regarding my fathering problem. I called and asked, but at first Pastor Sonya was hesitant. She said, "You are like a spiritual father to me, and yet you are asking me." So she had to pray about it first. But afterwards she agreed and I went to what we were thinking would be a two-hour session. Before you knew it we spent seven hours on an inner healing session. It went to different areas than I thought it would, and yet the greatest healing came from the love and gentleness of Pastor Sonya and her team. Along with the Spirit, they were used to bring healing to me in a profound way. The next week in Aruba, Pastor Sue Ahn mentioned that she saw something shifting in me and began asking me about it.

The next month the New Joy team went to Africa with me. While I carry the breakthrough anointing, Pastor Steven carries a father's anointing. The entire team knew how to position themselves as sons and daughters. On one of the first nights my neck was really tight. The massage therapist on the team offered to give a 10-minute neck rub. Instead, for an hour she just loved on me, massaged my sore neck, and shared her heart. The next day she came bubbling up and grabbed my arm and put her head on my shoulder and just loved on me every time she could. I didn't know what to do with it. One of the main issues Pastors David and Sonya had confronted me on was about stuffing my emotions and saying they are not important. This woman, Zana, had been used to stir up my emotions about something at the core of my heart. You see my daughter Loraina had gotten married a year and half before, and I had told myself she had to "leave and cleave." That was what I thought I was supposed to do, and it was true to some degree, but down deep inside I had shut something off emotionally. Now, God was using others to expose the wound. Zana tapped into that place and I admitted that I missed my natural daughter so much. I ran to my hotel room and called my daughter from Africa and told her how much I missed her. I told her that I was sorry for withdrawing so much and that I now saw that our relationship needed to be restored into a proper place. My goal here is to say this: don't let your wounds and coping as natural parents hinder you in the future. God wants to use spiritual sons and daughters to bring healing into your life.

On this trip, a most profound healing was happening in me. One of my most vivid memories was once when the whole team was sitting in a circle one morning. Everyone was sharing about their personal breakthroughs on the trip. A man about five years my elder was sitting next to me. Joel had positioned himself as a son to me and had accompanied Ann and me on trips around the world. Suddenly, faith hit me. I now have a greater ability in my heart to love on my sons in a way I never have. I stared at Joel's hand. It was so odd, I just wanted to grab it and show him affection, so I did. It didn't faze him. He acted like it was normal because we had such a great respect and love for each other. A woman on the trip who had traveled with me before said, "I don't even know who you are, what happened to you?" She was seeing a fathering side in me she had never seen before!

In essence, what I am telling you is that in the Kingdom there is an impartation to heal the fathers and the mothers. There is a movement of God coming into the church right now. I believe it is that the children are going to be the ones who heal the fathers and mothers, not just fathers and mothers healing the children! See Malachi 4:6, "He will turn the hearts of the parents to their children, and the hearts of the children to their parents..." Notice that it is a two way street; it is not only the hearts of the parents to their children, but the hearts of the children to their parents. When I got home from Africa, I went into my office and there were the two calls where people had called me "Papa." I had learned to show affection, and I told them I wanted to show them more love and took each of them out for lunch and just poured into them. One of them named Brooke came to me a couple of days later and told me something that gave me more revelation. She said, "I have not seen my father in five years. My siblings don't even want to see him. But, since you gave me so much of the Father's love this week, I feel differently. I feel that I can go to my father and expect nothing and actually be the one who goes to love on him. He needs my love." She got it, the daughter was going to go heal the father that was ashamed and rejected. She did, and her father wept and wept as she loved on him with a supernatural love.

The topic of apostolic fathering and mothering may be the hinge point that releases the body into a greater understanding of who we are called to be. It surely has been the key for me as I grew into my role as an apostle. It is deeply connected to being a father and embracing what that means in my role within the family of God.

At this point, I would like to shift into a related topic

that builds upon the principles of parenting in the Kingdom — apostolic alignment.

7

APOSTOLIC ALIGNMENT

My Baptist seminary taught the importance of autonomy in the local church. This was emphasized as a major tenet for leaders to remember. The denomination had input into our church, but ultimately they had no authority. As a young pastor, I found that this also created a tension between the church and the salaried pastors. The elder board (or whatever primary board name from your experience) expected the "hired gun" to do the ministry, but that had implied limits usually stated in the constitution or bylaws. Other limits were based on precedent and experience. In my first role as a senior pastor, the board let it be known that they had seen pastors come and go, but the church and its future belonged to them. In other words, autonomy implied that the pastor was dispensable!

This felt more like a tug of war than it did a spirit of cooperation. As long as I shared common goals and viewpoints, and worked toward that end, everything was fine. In other words, I was being told to "align" with them as my overseers. There is value in accountability, and I tried to work on this to the best of my ability. This context is called an elder-led church. Other churches are led by the senior leader, while others are ultimately congregational. This is the background and context that I was familiar with. From the very beginning of working within the churches, there was an underlying distrust of leaders. It wasn't that the people didn't have any trust or didn't respect me (or other leaders), but rather they had negative experiences that affected their attitude. In the three churches I served, two as senior pastor, I was often reminded of how controlling, insensitive, and disappointing other former leaders were. The predominant result was the leadership teams provided the "checks and balances" to keep the senior leader from abuse or too much control. In some ways this can be a positive thing, but when it's based on distrust and fear, it creates a unhealthy and dysfunctional environment.

I am sure this isn't true of all situations, but most traditional church pastors share this struggle openly when they get together. In my primary pastorate of 15 years, this actually improved and changed immensely as I was always honoring and cooperative with the Elder Board members. Regardless, I think it is safe to say that a lot of churches struggle with the tension between a board and its pastor.

When I started working in the context of HIM and with Harvest Rock Church, it displayed an entirely different model. The church ministry was led by Ché and Sue Ahn, and they functioned with the title of Senior Pastors. However, it was clearly understood by everyone that Ché and Sue were apostles. "This is an apostle-led church" was clearly communicated. Having served as a senior pastor with a lot of freedom, it still was radically different from what I saw at Harvest Rock Church. I am someone who has been to hundreds of churches in the past 12 years and I have met with many church boards and leadership teams. Regardless of the title, few churches run with one single primary leader such as an apostle. I believe this has to do with issues of trust and control, no matter what title the leaders have or what the government structure is. Frankly, it has been amazing to watch and be a part of an organization movement where the apostle is trusted and honored. Ché and Sue have grown and shifted as leaders over the years as everyone does. They are not perfect of course.

However, it has been an incredible journey to function in a church that is truly led by an apostle.

Let me talk personally for a moment. When we left our church of 15 years, I left with immense freedom while also leading a small network in Kenya. I had an elder board that recognized me as an apostle as well, but we still had residue of the old wineskin within our constitution. Even though I could function as I felt led, there was a part of me that knew that I didn't hold full authority and responsibility. Many think this may be the ideal approach, and certainly there is nothing wrong with team ministry. However, the scriptures are the authority, and when we compromise out of tradition, it does limit the power and effectiveness for the Kingdom.

God Has a Divine Order

In I Corinthians 12:28 it says, "And in the church God appointed first of all apostles, second prophets..." We looked at this earlier in the chapter on the biblical basis of apostleship. Elders are not the same as apostles, they are appointed by them. Overseers of local churches are to be in submission to them.

There I used it...the word "submission." In my former denomination, that was a word that no one liked to use. There was such an emphasis on plurality and equality. How dare we infer that someone has more authority? The problem was that people equated importance and value with authority. Thus, there was resistance to implying that anyone had to submit to anyone. I participated in this never wanting to infer that I had more authority than others. The problem is that it hurts the church. It causes God's appointed leaders to hold back in what they might think is healthy interdependence. The problem is that leaders need to lead. Now, I am not saying that leaders can't share authority, because they can. God told Moses to give some of his authority to Joshua, and it is amazing that we can do that. However, the authority did belong to Moses and everyone knew it. I believe that we see the apostles work as a team, and they listened and challenged one another.

Perhaps the best example of this is found in Galatians 2, when Paul challenged Peter about eating one way with Gentiles and another when around Jews. However, in that same chapter, it appears that James the brother of Jesus was clearly functioning as the presiding apostle. In addition, if someone does have the final authority, that doesn't remove the need or importance of accountability.

One of the words that other people have used is "covering." For some, this is a positive word that implies protection, blessing, and an umbrella-like safety. For others, the word covering has become an excuse for control or micro-management. The concept of covering is to infer that leaders are placed over us in authority by God to function as a conduit for blessing as well as a means of guarding us through this realm of authority sanctioned by God. We have had many people ask us to "cover" and bless them due to our role on the apostolic team of HIM. I understood their requests and considered it an honor.

With all this said, I do believe that honor is a two-way street, and that a good leader always keeps in mind and heart the needs of those appointed to them. However, I firmly believe that many churches that are not effective have a watered down view of authority. As an independent church leader, we felt quite isolated from the rest of the body of Christ. When we deviated from traditional Baptist theology and practice, we became a nuisance to the denomination. When we needed support and guidance, we learned that pastors were viewed as temporal and secondary leaders. Even when we were in good graces, the denomination had very little authority and influence in our church experience. The lack of leadership and true authority is probably a greater problem in the Body of Christ than the abuse of authority. The enemy has done everything he can do undermine the real authority God has instituted.

While we do not look down on the words "submission" and "covering," we prefer a different concept or word to describe our relationships and authority. While "submission" can be abused by position, and "covering" can lead to control, the word "alignment" has to do with the heart and how hearts are connected to one another. The word "alignment" is relational and functional. It describes how people respond and interact in their Kingdom relationships. The word "alignment" comes from Ephesians 4:12. The Greek word *katartismos* is usually translated "to equip" in the NIV and ESV, and "perfecting" in the KJV. It is important to connect it with the primary concept in that the fivefold leaders of Ephesians 4:11 equip the saints for works of ministry. Notice there is a connection or cause and effect stated here. Leaders have the authority and responsibility to equip the saints. The goal of any leader should be to equip and raise up others into their gifts and calling.

The word "equipping" is a medical term that refers to the setting of a broken bone so that it heals properly. When a bone is broken, it must be aligned properly for it to fuse correctly. Otherwise it can grow too small, or separate from the surrounding tissue, or bend in different directions. This often results in a need for corrective surgery where the bone actually needs to be broken again! Wow, this isn't a fun word at all. The picture of being broken like this isn't something that most people would find appealing. However, alignment is the process that God uses to hone all of us into the maturity and fullness that He has prepared for us. This verse is saying that if we are properly aligned, we will come into our destiny and purpose. If not, it will prevent us from being whom God called us to be!

What does this mean practically? It means that we are positioned in such a way that spiritual leaders can speak into our lives. There are those we entrust our hearts with and who will care for us and be able to speak into us with Godly wisdom and authority. These leaders have the responsibility to mold, guide, and impart what is necessary for each person to grow into their fivefold and broader purpose. The word "equip" is about developing relationships where spiritual leaders are able to train and release us throughout development stages.

This does speak to the character and maturity of the leaders, that is, their ability to duplicate and equip others. However, alignment infers that those who want to grow demonstrate an attitude of alignment. This implies that they desire and seek out mentors, spiritual parents, and fivefold leaders to equip them. As a local church pastor for over 24 years, I often found that people think and operate independently from leaders. I used to joke that ministry was like herding cats. Some of that could have been a lack of leadership on my part, but it also had to do with the overall view toward leadership that I described earlier. Leaders were often viewed with doubt, suspicion, and distrust. How painful for everyone. It takes faith for leaders and followers alike to believe in one another. This is the core of what alignment is about, it takes faith that God aligns us with leaders and communities.

Alignment in Practice

Doug and Debbie Healy are pastors who started a church in Orange County, California over 13 years ago. Over the years, they longed for alignment, but didn't know exactly where to turn. They went to different hot spots of the Kingdom, and received a lot of training and impartation. However, they did not feel like they had spiritual parents that knew them personally. They couldn't express what they needed exactly, but they knew they needed a deeper connection than being a part of conferences and training events. This is what a need for alignment feels like. It goes to the place in our hearts where God designed us to be—spiritually aligned with those He purposed. This, in part, is why we are called a body. Each part is important and connected to other parts strategically. Many people never come into their full purpose and calling simply because they are not aligned properly in the body.

In the Fall of 2014, Doug attended a conference at HRock Church. When he saw Ché Ahn in front at one of the services, the Spirit said to him, "Ché Ahn is your spiritual father." The next day Doug went to the information meeting to find out how to join the Harvest International Ministry Network. That's where he and I met. From there, the snowball rolled as Ann and I went to their church several times. We bonded deeply. Doug accompanied me to Mexico and God confirmed strongly that we were being aligned. It is interesting to note here that Doug and Debbie were becoming aligned with Ché Ahn through Ann and me. In other words, they were aligned through Ché Ahn's son and daughter. Doug and Debbie testify that this alignment has dramatically impacted their personal lives as well as their entire church. We have grown closer and closer, and it has been a joy to see the favor that is upon their lives. Since aligning they have had a merger with a ministry that is providing a building for them! Their attendance has nearly doubled and so is their influence in building the region. They are also now leading the Mexico trips to Tijuana that are uniting and impacting the city. They are growing as apostles and have gone to a new level of ministry. They have impacted our lives as well, their love and honor has overwhelmed us at times.

As the former Executive Director of HIM, my primary

role was to minister to our members as well as develop relationships with those inquiring about our network. Then, as I was released into my current role as the Missions Apostle, this escalated to more of a global role. Time and time again I hear testimonies of people that saw a measurable and tangible increase in their ministry in terms of momentum, purpose, finances, and sense of belonging in the larger body of Christ. This is the power of alignment.

When the Doug and Debbie went on the Mexico trip the next year, they came to Ann and me and said, "We have something to tell you. God has persuaded us to align our hearts with you as a father and mother. We want to love and serve you in any way we can." The next year, they led the trip to Mexico and Ann and I went to support and relate to the apostolic leaders of Tijuana. This alignment freed Ann and me to go to another level in our call, as they also were raised up in theirs.

As I shared earlier, my denominational family saw me as a misfit as they saw us change in a radical way. We didn't know where to turn, but like many others, we started going to conferences to learn and grow from others that had the same heart. We went to Pasadena, California because my parents lived close by and it helped us afford going to such events. We did this for over six years, until we received a word from the Lord to join HIM. We partially remained in our denomination up until then and also for a couple of years after we joined the network. When we became aligned with HIM, we did start to see a shift. Ché Ahn visited our church and he said he sensed a poverty spirit. I know in hindsight I contributed to that. He stood up and broke the poverty mindset and released a blessing of generosity. He taught us how to give in a more honoring way to the Lord as well as to those who came and ministered in our midst. The next year we saw an increase in giving of over 60%. We knew that it was a spiritual blessing that came through alignment with Ché (as our apostle) and

HIM.

When Ché asked me to become the Executive Director, which I shared earlier in this book, people from my church asked me how I would work under someone else? They believed I was a very strong leader and could have my own apostolic ministry. I feel very confident that I could go on my own and lead my own network like I did in Kenya before I joined HIM. However, this is worldly thinking. Being number one in your ministry is not the goal for everyone. One day I asked the Lord my spiritual name and he told me "Caleb." At the time I didn't focus on the fact that he was not number one in authority. I was a young pastor taking people out of tradition into the "promised land" of spiritual renewal and freedom. Later on, I realized that when I accepted being under Ché Ahn that I was fulfilling my role as Caleb.

My role and sphere of authority is far beyond what it could ever be on my own. We are in over 60 nations, and last year I was in 16 of them. This is all due to proper alignment. At this time, I have no desire to be my own man or ministry. God may shift the needs of HIM or me personally someday, but during this past 12 years, it has been the essence of me coming into my purpose and destiny. I call it the apostolic train, when the leader goes forward so does everyone connected to him on the train. Of course, Jesus our foremost alignment. However, He does send us others to align with as well.

I love being aligned with Ché and Sue Ahn. They believe in Ann and me and have been extremely supportive and invested in us. Have we had any issues? Yes, of course, but none that we were not able to work through. Ann and I understand the value and importance of alignment. We value different realms and spheres of authority. We don't hold judgment toward leaders if they have another approach or priorities different from what we think they should be. We focus on our realm and submit that with joy to our spiritual parents and leaders. Alignment is a choice; it involves covenant and commitment.

Recently, I realized that I had been ignoring my health due to all my travels. I took an honest look at my eating habits and other patterns that were impacting my health. So I asked them for a sabbatical to focus on my physical health. Their response was immediate and so affirming that it went deep into my spirit. They cared about me more than anything else. Do you know that proper alignment can lead to the most profound healing and sense of security? Ché and Sue don't have time to just hang out all of the time, so don't interject that here. Our times of fellowship are not regular, and can be as few as four or five times a year. The alignment is in our hearts, and we don't have false expectations. Busy world changers and fivefold leaders are not going to be there to walk us through everything. That comes down to having partners and friends as well. Alignment has to do with proper spiritual authority and blessing in our lives. Alignment is an essential component to relational transformation. In fact, it is directly related to the expansion of spheres of influence and effectiveness. If you are called to be an apostolic leaders with people aligned with you, you must be aligned yourself. In other words, you can't ask them to do what you are not living out in your own life.

Partners, Friends, or Ministry Relationships?

I believe that many people are frustrated and disappointed because they don't understand the difference between partners, friends, and ministry relationships. It is unhealthy to expect all of our friends to be partners, and all our partners to be our friends. There is not enough time in the day to do this. Also, some relationships we have were never intended to be reciprocal or life-giving to us. Some of the people we minister to are drowning and need to be the focus. When we apply this to alignment, don't put false expectations of what it means to be in relationship. We are aligned with Jesus, He is the source of everything we need to sustain and strengthen us. God uses leaders with whom we are aligned: friends, partners, and other people to give us what we need to mature and grow. When it comes down to it, alignment is in the heart.

Here is an important question. Are most people aligned properly? I don't believe they are. Many leaders feel disconnected and alone in their quest to serve God. Earlier, I mentioned the orphan heart as it relates to spiritual fathers and mothers. However, when we apply the characteristics of an orphan heart, it reveals the tendency to not be aligned with leaders. This is because an independent spirit sabotages intimacy and creates distance due to mistrust, emotional stifling and self-protection. This, in turn, exacerbates feelings of abandonment and loneliness. I remember as a pastor how rejected and undervalued I felt by the denominational leaders. I blamed others as being unfaithful and unsupportive. Ungodly beliefs grew in my spirit, "I have to do it myself. No one really cares or understands. Others help because they are obligated." I was defensive, and had a tendency to overreact when I was threatened or slighted in my mind.

For some, when they think of authority figures, it is a source of pain or agitation. It makes it hard to trust the words of those with authority as being sincere. It comes down to the basic slave or servant mentality vs. the feeling of a love and accepted son or daughter. That is a terrible place to be in as a leader. I believe that we are living in a time where most people feel that they have not been mentored or have had spiritual parents. Many don't know whom to be aligned with, even if they wanted to.

Perhaps this is a reflection of the culture in which we

have an epidemic of those without natural fathers and mothers. We live in a time where people want to be independent, and actually do not want to learn from the parents, but do it on their own. They want to learn from their own mistakes, and actually many young adults have rejected the ways of their parents. This has led to a lack of honor, not only by the children, but by the parents too. In the body of Christ, the church has often lost the ability to mentor and disciple. Many churches have the goal of attracting more and more people, but do not take responsibility or have a vision to help people grow and come into their destiny. However, I have good news. This is what the apostolic movement is about—alignment for everyone. There is a move of God coming into the church and we see it around the world. In part, there is a restoration of fathering and mothering in the Body of Christ. But alignment takes it a step further, as it defines the roles and a way that a person functions in the midst of these relationships.

Right now, God is bringing us into a new alignment with one another. So how does this take place? This isn't intended to be the order, but here are some basic principles on how alignment happens.

Start with inner healing. He is becoming the restored lover of our heart and being. There are more opportunities for inner healing then ever before. So, to be properly aligned, we need to make the fundamental pursuits. God is called to be our first love and it starts with Him. We can't look to people to meet needs that only He can meet. Do everything you can do deal with everything that separates you in your own mind from the love of the Father. Romans 8:14-17 says:

"For those who are led by the Spirit of God are the children of God. The Spirit you received does not make you slaves, so that you live in fear again; rather, the Spirit you

received brought about your adoption to sonship. And by him we cry, Abba, Father. The Spirit himself testifies with our spirit that we are God's children. Now if we are children, then we are heirs—heirs of God and co-heirs with Christ, if indeed we share in his sufferings in order that we may also share in his glory."

To be properly aligned, first we must walk in this. We need to overcome all fear, condemnation, and a slavery mentality. We are co-heirs with Christ. Isn't it amazing—what belongs to him, belongs to us! Jesus said in John 17 that he had given us the same glory that the Father gave to him. Our relationship with God can be the same as Jesus had.

We need to learn how to call God, "Daddy." If we can't, it means that we have suffered abandonment, rejection, worthlessness, or insecurity with our real fathers. Pursue inner healing with all your heart.

Next, we must honor our father and mother regardless of what we think they have or have not done for us. We must release them from our judgments and false expectations. We need to have restoration and reconciliation with our fathers and mothers. This principle can't be skipped or downplayed. None of us had perfect parents, so there are offenses and hurts that simply are a result of our sinful nature. This process of learning to honor them is vital for a release of blessing into our lives. In essence, we the children need to turn our hearts to our father and mothers even before they turn them to us.

Finally, acknowledge and recognize whom God wants you to be aligned with as spiritual fathers and mothers. God wants to put you into alignment with leaders who speak into our lives. If you don't know who that is to be, pray with a focus on this. Ask the Lord to show you what to do. I am a firm proponent of networks, obviously since I am a leader in one. The reason is that I believe the fivefold is God's design to incorporate the diversity and needs of the body for spiritual connection and alignment. If you want to come into your purpose, you need to find role models who can impart and release the truths into your life. As you mature, that is your call as well. It is very difficult to know how to have people align with us when we don't know how to do it ourselves. The reason I am writing this is to assist churches and ministers to have a vision for this. A lot of churches say they have a heart for merging the generations. I believe that teaching proper alignment is central to this desire to unite the generations.

Who are you aligned with? Are you accountable to a leader? Do you give anyone real spiritual authority and oversight in your life? If you can't say "yes" to this, you are not properly aligned. Go through the order, with the heavenly Father on the top followed by our natural parents then with spiritual leaders. You will see a pattern that you may or may not like. You may be a sincere Christian leader who wants to make a difference. However, as gifted as you may be, without alignment, it is very difficult to sustain enough traction to grow in influence and authority. This is why Jesus chose the model of raising up 12 apostles. It is the foundation, as Ephesians 2:20 clearly says, "built on the foundation of the apostles and prophets, with Christ Jesus himself as the chief cornerstone." I believe this is a profound picture that gives us a glimpse of how to build and grow, and it's through alignment.

Earlier, I made a reference to the blended word "glocal." This is a word that captures the application of alignment in the New Testament. As we know, the early church was centered around Jerusalem. As the church grew around the region and the world, there was an ongoing relationship with the church there. That is where the apostles gathered for leadership meetings and summits as they sought to oversee and respond to the needs of the growing movement. In addition, the apostles in Jerusalem sent out leaders to various regions as the needs arose.

How did the Early Church Align and Relate?

This was a two way relationship that demonstrated how alignment functioned in the early church. For example in Acts 8:14 we are told, "When the apostles in Jerusalem heard that Samaria had accepted the Word of God, they sent Peter and John to Samaria." The purpose was to provide needed support and blessing from the founding and key leaders. In Acts 15, there were teachers who were causing division and confusion over the topic of circumcision. The action they took was an understanding of alignment as seen in Acts 15:2, "This brought Paul and Barnabas into sharp dispute and debate with them. So, Paul and Barnabas were appointed, along with some other believers, to go up to Jerusalem to see the apostles and elders about this question." Notice the practice or procedure that was intact, as it reflects a basic flow of communication that was reciprocal. In response to this inquiry, the apostles replied by sending some leaders along with Paul and Barnabas. This is recorded in Acts 15:22-23, then the apostles and elders, with the whole church, decided to choose some of their own men and send them to Antioch with Paul and Barnabas. They chose Judas (called Barsabbas) and Silas, men who were leaders among the believers. With them they sent a letter. In the letter they said something that reveals the authority that was recognized and honored. In Acts 15:24 it says, "We have heard that some went out from us without our authorization and disturbed you, troubling your minds by what they said." This shows a high level of accountability, and all the more powerful, the leaders in Jerusalem took responsibility and initiated this communication out of concern for the local church that was aligned with them.

This points to an important truth about alignment, those who are in leadership need to have their hearts "aligned" with those they serve. This is consistent with the medical image of a broken bone, there are two sides that need to align. All too often leaders have expected people to honor them, without showing a mutual respect toward those they cover or lead.

In Acts 16:4-5, we can see that the benefits of alignment with the Jerusalem church leaders:

> *"As they traveled from town to town, they delivered the decisions reached by the apostles and elders in Jerusalem for the people to obey. So the churches were strengthened in the faith and grew daily in numbers."*

I want to emphasize that this "Glocal" relationship gave immense strength to the local church by giving foundational support of the movement. This is how alignment works according to God's design.

Further ahead in Acts 16:4-5 we can see the authority and benefits being aligned with the Jerusalem church leaders, "As they traveled from town to town, they delivered the decisions reached by the apostles and elders in Jerusalem for the people to obey. So the churches were strengthened in the faith and grew daily in numbers." I want to emphasize that this glocal relationship gave immense strength to the local church by giving foundational support of the movement. This is how alignment works according to God's design.

At present, HIM has churches in over 60 nations, and this concept of global and local alignment brings the same kind of strength to what God is doing around the world. It is not our desire to control anything, but leaders around the world look to us to encourage, bless, validate, and strengthen their ministry. I am not implying that we are the Jerusalem, as there are other great leadership hubs and bases that are doing the same kind of work around the world. However, local leaders want the sense that they are a part of what God is doing in other nations. When I go to a nation, I don't view it as hierarchical, but rather the global is called to honor and respect the local. However, these leaders want to know if what they are doing is consistent with other leaders and movements around the world. They also want to receive impartation, prayer, and practical support that is available through global apostles. This is how alignment works in a larger setting and brings unity in the body around the world.

8

MASTER EQUIPPERS

This chapter is dedicated to the topic of being a master equipper. I don't believe that the equipping takes place automatically, just as someone doesn't get pregnant by just being in the same room as another person. That may seem as an extreme example but I think we take the importance of intentionally equipping too lightly. It takes time to work with others, to blend and make sure that we are on the same page, and to work through our differences. As a senior pastor, I was expected to do a lot of the work in the church. I preached virtually every Sunday morning, led Bible studies, organized small group programs and recruited volunteers for children and youth programs. As the church grew, I had to rely more on volunteers. We eventually hired additional staff. Without really choosing it, we as leaders generally saw ourselves doing the main work of the ministry. Volunteers that were dedicated and assertive were able to work into various roles, and we greatly appreciated it. But we weren't intentionally seeking to release people into their passions.

I want to underscore here that I believe fivefold ministers and leadership need to view their primary function as equippers. The more mature a leader becomes the greater their ability to duplicate and raise up others into their purpose and calling. To really do this, we need to believe that each person has purpose ordained by God. Just as the Lord declared over Jeremiah, "Before you born I set you apart!" Fivefold leaders are raised up by the Spirit to prepare God's people for works of service, that is ministry. To do, this leaders must have the ability to discern God's greater plan for each person. This is why I am so committed to the fivefold; I view it as a blueprint for every person. Everybody wants to know what they were created for, and while in ministry I was often asked by people what I thought their purpose was. It wasn't until I came into an understanding of the fivefold ministry that this began to grow in my spirit and become a greater priority.

The more I study the life and ministry of Jesus, it is amazing to see his desire to give away his ministry all along the way. The very choice of the word "apostle" was an indication that Jesus was preparing these leaders to be sent out as ambassadors with this authority that he carried. This transfer, or impartation, is the model that Jesus demonstrated and lived out. So I needed to admit that this was not modeled to me by my mentors and it wasn't something that I saw as my first and foremost priority. However, if we take Ephesians 4:12 seriously, it implies that every fivefold leader wants to make this among their primary goals. In the last chapter we reviewed alignment, which looks at the positioning of hearts and relationships in ministry. However, this does not tell us how people are actually equipped.

This takes place in a variety of settings and methods, but it starts with a heart of the leader. It takes a commitment to give away the ministry, that is, to share it in a way so others can contribute in a significant way. Often in a church people are offered roles that help the day to day functions to meet the basic means for church services and the maintenance of programs. Since the church is like a family, it has basic needs related to the building, preparation and cleanup, and there are many important tasks necessary to function. So this becomes a priority for recruiting volunteers, and as any and pastor can tell you it's not always easy to recruit people just to meet the essential needs of the congregation.

Obstacles to Equipping

While all those helps are important, I'm not sure anyone feels that their main purpose in life is to prepare bulletins or to work in the nursery. Again, these things are important and must be done. So please don't think I'm discounting their value and necessity. As the church grows larger, these tasks are often met by hired people, mainly because they are consistent and it is easier for communication and expectations. Volunteers are to be treated differently than employees, and as we know both employees and volunteers are critical for any organization to exist. Among leaders, there is an understanding that around 10% of the congregation will do a 90% of the work. Another obstacle to equipping for me was that I was taught that I should seek God and get a vision for the church. As the primary leader, I had that responsibility placed on me and I took it upon my shoulders. In turn, I shared that with key leaders around me, and I patiently waited for them to assess it and have the opportunity to confirm or redirect the vision. However, as I changed into the apostolic role, I became uncomfortable with this model. It seemed so church-oriented as it related to my vision. We would go before the church and share the revelation and vision we received from God, and called people to fulfill it and to become supporters in accomplishing its goals. This approach has value, as it is important to keep the corporate vision in front of the people and to set goals as a community. But deep inside, I realized something had to change.

After going to Kenya the first year, I came home frustrated with the local church. The main reason was because it seemed like those in Africa had a lot more spiritual hunger, and they were eager to seek the Lord for their lives.

At home, it appeared as though people were just too busy, and it was a major effort just to take care of their crowded schedules, work demands and family needs. I actually felt guilty asking people to do things because I didn't want to take them away from their family. I was partly right, but at the core I was missing the point. Sometimes the church served the people, but other times it took advantage of the few that were willing to give and serve. Consequently, the burnout rate was high as well as the turnover. There were a few who hung in there and were willing to do anything, but often I would hear from their spouses who wished they spent more time at home. This is when I realized, that a big part of the problem is how I did church. It was unlike what we did on the mission trips, and it was the leadership that needed to change. To put it bluntly, it revealed that equipping was not at the core of our approach. In time, I publicly repented, because I realized that the way I approached church was quite selfish. I didn't do this on purpose, however we were more focused on people coming into our vision, and much less about the people coming into their vision and what they are created for. This had to change, and I started with my own perspective and heart as the senior leader.

Sending Out in Pairs

In the second trip to Kenya I took a team with me, and found that there was much opportunity; I could send them out in pairs like Jesus did. Often it was in groups of two, sometimes it was three or four and they would go out to a village for an entire day. The folks on my team had all types of backgrounds. Very few had attended a Bible school of any kind. They just wanted to serve Jesus and be a part of something bigger than they had been before.

Some things happened right in front of my eyes. Members would come back to the hotel changed and challenged in radical ways. Suddenly they couldn't look to me as the hired gun to fulfill their needs...they were it! I gave them very basic training. For example, I had them write down three or four major areas where God had worked in their lives. I then asked them to study verses around those experiences, and suddenly they have a sermon message based on personal testimony. I also taught them how to pray for the sick, and how to persevere in faith when they didn't see results. In other words, I just gave them the basic skills and sent them out to wherever we were requested to go. The need outweighed the amount of people that we had, so we could send teams out all over the region. People would come back to the hotel, and ask, "What do I teach tomorrow?" I would tell them to pray and talk to other team members and see what is in their hearts and then share it. The team members would come back so excited, and tell me, "It was amazing how God orchestrated the day." This kind of sentiment has become normal in these cases; I literally have sent out hundreds of teams over the years, and reports like this are common.

Some people that would go on the trip would tell me at the beginning, "I don't want to speak in front of people." So I decided to present them with three different categories. I outlined the three different categories and then asked people to raise their hands for the one that best described them. First, there are the people who would like to start off in the background. They're willing to pray for people one-on-one, intercede during the meeting, and assist with logistics. Second group; these are those who are ready to share a brief testimony as well as to participate in a supportable way. The third category...these are the ones who are eager to teach or preach from the beginning, confident enough to lead a meeting or a section of one. It is very important for people to choose what they think they are able to do from the start. The reason is I want people to know that it is not my goal for everyone to be in the third group. It is my goal that everyone feels like they grow and have freedom to explore who they are in Christ and to discover the gifts that they have. So I tell the group, "I don't expect everyone to get up in front and talk, I just want everyone to know that you are important and I believe God will use each one in a unique and significant way."

In 2014, Pastor Joe's wife, Andrea, went with us to Mexico. He had gone on the trip with me to Africa earlier that year. She had seen such a change in him that she wanted to be a part of a trip as well. She told me right away that she did not like to speak in front of people. Andrea has a great heart and she loves people, but she said she was actually afraid to get in front of people. I think my answer surprised her, because I immediately took away that expectation. I told her I just wanted her to have fun, and to feel like she had freedom to do what was on her heart. I encouraged her to come to me if she had something that she wanted to do and I would try to make it possible. For the first few days she blended in, and contributed in a comfortable way. Turns out that Andrea has a lot of wisdom, and she sees things that others miss. She also feels the heart of God deeply for others. So, during one meeting, as the team was sharing, she felt that she had something she needed to share with the people. An opportunity came for her, and she got up and encouraged the people for a moment, then sat down. During the next week, Andrea felt no pressure and participated as she was led. Several times she shared in churches, but most often prayed for people and encouraged as many as possible. She stretched herself by going out with the evangelism teams on the streets. When she returned home the next weekend, she volunteered to share what God had done to her in Mexico in the Sunday Service. Her husband, along with the other pastors, were shocked because Andrea had been unwilling, or perhaps even unable, to share in front of the congregation before.

Now, she was volunteering to report in the morning service, and when she did, there was so much momentum and life in her heart that she followed the leading of the Spirit to do the morning message! The next day her husband called and asked me, "What happened to my wife on this trip!? She is a changed person." While this illustration may seem like an example that is extreme, it really isn't. When people are in an environment of freedom and encouragement, it is common to see them have major breakthroughs. As 2 Corinthians 3:17 says, "Where the Spirit of the Lord is there is freedom."

In addition to freedom, another key to equipping people is to listen to the burdens on their hearts. God has designed all of us uniquely and perfectly. When God spoke to Jeremiah, He declared over him, "I set you apart before you were born." If we press into the meaning of this, we can see that God has prepared wonderful things for us and they are part of who we are. The burdens and the passions that we have are an indication of what we are destined to bring the life of the Spirit to. This is why I'm so committed to the fivefold ministry. It is like a blueprint that reveals how God has created a ministry emphasis into our hearts that is woven deeply into our creation. Therefore, I encourage every leader to learn not only the primary fivefold ministries in their own life, but how to recognize that in the lives of others.

A few years ago on a trip to Israel, there was a woman named Lisa from Singapore who joined our group of over 50 people. She heard Papa Ché speak and wanted to be a part of the trip. During meal times I heard her encourage other people with what felt like words from the Lord. She never said it, but you could tell it was coming from discernment and wisdom in the Spirit. When I had the opportunity, I spoke to her and shared that I believe she had a prophetic anointing. She responded with surprise and told me that no one had ever said that before. Then she asked, "How do I learn more about this?" I invited her to join us on our trip to India and told her that she would grow in the prophetic and learn how to move in it freely. So she went on the trip with us to Nepal and India, and she was trained and released like everyone else on the team. Lisa was a natural, she flowed in the Spirit and was filled with compassion for the people. I saw her growing in her gifting, and she became more comfortable with flowing in it. At the end of the trip, I asked her how many people she thought she prophesied over. Without blinking an eye she said, "Probably over 1,000 people."

This brings me to a third aspect on the subject of equipping people. They have to have an opportunity to apply what they're learning. It is common for people to take classes and to learn a great deal about spiritual things, but there is little opportunity to practice and participate in a significant way. It is true that we have to measure a person's ability and to match it with an appropriate setting. We can't just let anyone share on a Sunday morning or release them as a trainer without measurable ways to verify their gifting. This is why I love taking people to developing nations, as there are thousands of villages that are blessed just to have any guests come to them. They always say that it makes them feel like God has not forgotten them. In these settings, the people are so hungry and eager that they often walk over two miles to come to a meeting. Some of the sharing is very basic and simple, but it is so encouraging to the people because they feel God's love and hear His truth. In addition to all of our teams focus on how to give words of strength and encouragement, we invite people for prayer for salvation and healing. Just recently, I took a team to Northern India; we went to several villages and we saw over 50 people come to Christ and six totally deaf people healed, and this was in two days! Such an experience can change your life forever. Of course you can grow in other settings, but it is important to be a part of a ministry that releases people into the fivefold ministry.

As you've read this book, there is an intentional build up to this chapter. Alignment and spiritual parenting create an atmosphere for releasing people into their gifts and purpose. This is the primary goal of the relational transformation. I encourage people to be in relationship with others who can speak and impart into their life. Equipping takes place in the context of relationships and accountability over the long run. There are many gifted people who've felt they have not been moving in their calling. The main reason is they are disconnected. As I have led trips, there have been very strong people come on them, but they were struggling with rejection as it relates to church leaders.

On one trip to Kenya, we had a very strong evangelist. She reached out to the workers on the beach, some in prostitution and others working with the hotels. She started a service early in the morning right there on the sand as the workers got off. She recruited team members to join her and they had an amazing baptism service right there. However, when it came to team meetings and fitting into as a whole, it was very difficult for her. She had important things to do, and felt less effective if she had to go and sit in what she perceived to be non-essential meetings. As the team leader, it is my goal to unite us in our purpose, protect the team members, and communicate the larger vision in such meetings. My flesh wanted to simply confront her and tell her how important the meetings were, but the Lord gave me a different strategy. I went to her and affirmed her amazing evangelistic gift, and shared that I was excited about her impartation to the team members. I communicated that these meetings we have were for the purpose of imparting our gifts and valuing one another. So when she came to the next session, I intentionally affirmed her publicly to hear testimony of what God had been doing through her. At the end of the trip, she came to me and said, "I have never been fathered before. I'm usually misunderstood." She thanked me for accepting and loving her. Equipping is not simply teaching people what they need to know, but rather it is more about creating a culture where we acknowledge and honor one another's gifts.

A short term mission trip is great for opportunity, but long-term relationships have a greater impact. This is where alignment and spiritual parenting come in. Well after a trip has ended, we hear from people who move on into other ministry situations, and being connected with others is their greatest battle. It isn't that they do not know their gifts, but they don't know where and how to sustain and grow in them on an ongoing basis. This is why God designed the church! It is supposed to be the greenhouse for everyone to flourish.

In previous generations, people had to go to Bible college or seminary to get their advanced training. But now, there has been an incredible increase to receive a variety of powerful training and equipping events. There are schools of the supernatural, Wagner University (formerly Wagner Leadership Institute), weekly conferences, and excellent classes offered within the local churches. In our apostolic center, it is amazing to see the diversity and quality of the training contexts. If a person is hungry and willing to learn and grow, the opportunities are endless. The next step however is activation and application. Knowledge and experience are not the same thing, and while we need practical knowledge, there needs to be a plan to explore these new truths. To equip them is far more than simply training, it must involve contexts where these truths can become a reality. The Lord has been speaking to me about the apostolic transformation, and one of the primary emphases I hear is that true change is sustainable. It isn't something that just happens once, or is infrequent. If we just have events and meetings and endless activities, it doesn't mean that anything sustainable has been established. This is why equipping is such a significant topic, because it is about helping others transition into ministries and lifestyles that have measurable and sustainable results.

9

WHERE DO WE GO FROM HERE?

As Ann and I visit churches and ministries around the world, we marvel at the diversity of expressions that appear. No longer are leaders compelled to have a traditional church that follows a predictable pattern. That isn't to say there aren't lots of similarities; of course there are. However, as leaders discover their individual gifts and anointings, they realize that it is more effective to specialize and focus.

Let me share a case study of a ministry that has morphed with different forms to illustrate. Steven and Rene Springer were saved by a radical encounter with God outside the four walls of the church. Deeply desiring for others to encounter God's love and the power of His spirit, their home became a gathering place centered on God's presence through worship and prayer. As ministry to and from the heart of God was aligned in their lives, the ministry "Global Presence" was birthed.

In 2008, they began a unique expression of a house of prayer with a missional community entitled, "The Furnace." Its goal was to seek the presence of God and cry out for the city and region. They secured a building very close to the University of Wisconsin Campus and opened the doors for people to come and pray. Over a period of time, this led to doing some basic training on prayer, how to worship as a lifestyle, intercession, spiritual warfare, and supernatural evangelism. There was never an inkling that this move of God would become a "kind-of-church."

You see, both Steven and Rene knew they couldn't do a traditional church, and neither one had a great desire to pastor. However, they determined that if they stayed true to who they were as apostolic and prophetic leaders, they could also raise up the other fivefold, including pastoral leaders to shepherd the flock.

With an emphasis on the apostolic, the house of prayer remained the heartbeat of the ministry. For the Springers, the presence of the Lord is not the benefit, it is the essence of who they are and from which everything flows. Not ever wanting to pattern the "church" after what they knew, it actually was a training center which released people into their destiny, creativity, and freedom. As the Spirit led, they kept true to who they were personally, and released others to do the same. In time the word "church" felt limiting and too narrow. The local ministry blossomed into many expressions; an art gallery, an in-house fitness center, a dance studio, a legal clinic, a marketplace with business development resources, a healing center, and other exciting ministries. On the global scene, they were led to Ghana, where they were given land. They developed a world changing Transformation Center. As a hub, they realized that they were an "Apostolic Center."

I asked the Springers just when and how did they know that they were called to be an apostolic center? They replied:

> *"In 2003, during a fasting time, we heard the Lord speak about establishing an apostolic hub. We had never heard that term before and just started proceeding toward that. I knew that we were going to have five full houses of prayer with miracles, signs and wonders, and media. It was 2009 when we started saying we were an*